M000265880

*Books by Rollie McKenna*

Rollie McKenna: A Life in Photography    1991

Portrait of Dylan: A Photographer's Memoir    1982

Harbor Tug by Peter Burchard
    Photographs by Rollie McKenna    1975

The Modern Poets: An American-British Anthology
    Edited by John Malcolm Brinnin and Bill Read
    Photographs by Rollie McKenna    1963, 1970

# ROLLIE McKENNA

# A Life in Photography

*Photographs following:*

iv

# ROLLIE McKENNA

# A Life in Photography

*Foreword by* Richard Wilbur

Alfred A. Knopf   *New York*   1991

*Foreword by* Richard Wilbur

IT MAY BE that the best photographs are those which do not speak at once of the photographer's selectivity and craft. On first looking at them, we are so taken by the subject as to be unmindful of art: we see something, and to some extent see into it, as if the only agency were our own mysteriously heightened powers of perception. Rollie McKenna's pictures enable me in that way, and so does the spare, presentational prose in which she tells her life story. This photographer, who is so little drawn to taking self-portraits, does not crop her memories into an obvious series of formative events; but her engaging narrative lets us glimpse, again and again, how it was that she found her way.

One sees how her early life, which might well have made her insecure, resulted instead in self-reliance and that talent for being "happily neglected" which is indispensable to any artist; how a tomboy girlhood gave her a taste for freedom and adventure; how her grandparents set her a happy example by their industry and their power to cope; how Grandma Bacon schooled her in observation, while her architect grandfather gave her a structural sense of buildings; how, as a hotel-dwelling child, she early encountered people of every class and kind, and developed a relish for human variety . . . and so on, until, by way of fine arts study at Vassar, and the museums of Europe, she came at last—in Paris, in 1948—to the fated purchase of her first camera.

There is very little said in this book about photographic technique, most of it being relegated to a note at the end. It goes without saying that her pictures of the Ghiberti doors, for example, are proof of the greatest technical mastery; yet that is not, for her, the supreme thing. (How could it be, for an artist who can say that the camera, under some circumstances, is "an obstacle to seeing"?) The supreme thing is insight, and the chief motive of her superb shot of the domes of San Marco, taken from the top of the campanile, is that she knows, and wishes to show in one frame, how the church is put together.

Though the makeup of persons is more elusive than that of buildings, the portraits are similarly motivated by insight, and some of this book's best words about picture-taking concern the sort of timing required if the shutter is to open to the opening subject. I was reminded, in reading them, of what Ingemar Johansson, training for a championship bout with Floyd Patterson, once said to a *Times* reporter. When, the reporter asked, did Johansson plan to throw his celebrated right—when he saw an opening? "If I see the opening," Johansson replied, "it's too late. The right sees the opening." The portrait photographer, McKenna says, needs a similar Zen-like capacity to decide before deciding, to act before the decision comes fully to consciousness. This sort of distributed awareness, "coordinating muscle and sensibility" to capture the moment of self-revelation, came naturally, I suppose, to one who had been a quick-handed tennis player and an expert pistolshot.

What's wrong with such comparisons, of course, is that fists, racquets and pistols are aggressive things, whereas a refusal to coerce or to use the intimidations of the studio are part of the genius of Rollie McKenna's portrait work. When she first came out to South Lincoln to take my picture, in 1951, I was at once greatly relieved to find her winsome, comradely, and humorous. We crossed the road to a cow-pasture, on whose suggestion I don't recall; I sat down on a fallen tree, and she, in pursuit of the right slant or composition, straddled an up-angled dead branch and began hitching backward on it toward the sky. That took my mind off myself almost entirely, and it is amusing to read in this book how similar antics, in a window-recess or on a garden wall, later disarmed such diffident subjects as T. S. Eliot and David Gascoyne.

Self-forgetfulness in the photographer is contagious and can with luck call forth a truer self. The people in McKenna's portraits are all posing to some extent, and not all are smiling, yet almost all are responding to a benign concentration and a friendliness which is not intrusive. Even Ezra Pound, prompted by these things and by a blameless trick, surfaces for a moment from the depression of his later years. The world of Rollie McKenna's portraits, for all the diversity and difficulty of her subjects, is (thanks to her) a warm and sociable one.

# Contents

# ROLLIE McKENNA

# A Life in Photography

# The South
## 1918–1931

*We Enchanted Our Guests*

Henry Sanford Thorne
c. 1917

C HILDHOOD conditioned me to an unconventional life. Parents and grandparents came and went, uncles substituted for brothers, aunts for sisters, and a constantly changing panorama of people and events taught me that independence did not necessarily mean neglect. At times I was not certain to whom I belonged or even who I was, but there was always someone to turn to or something to do. In a sense I was everybody's child, exposed to adult situations not customarily allowed. At sixteen I was my own person. Though "genetically endowed" with a photographic propensity by two great-grandparents I never knew and exposed to painting and architecture by two grandparents in my youth, it was not until I was thirty-two that I decided to become a photographer.

Four days after the end of the First World War, I was born to Bel Bacon Thorne and Henry Thorne in Houston, Texas. A few months later we left Camp Gerstner, where my father had become a pilot in the Army Air Corps, so that he could resume his studies at Yale University.

My parents liked the name Rosalie. And since my last name was Thorne, they called me "Rollie," to avoid "Rose" or "Rosie." When I found my profession, many people assumed that my nickname was spelled "Rollei," short for Rolleiflex, the popular camera I frequently used, or "Rolly" which is sometimes short for Roland. However misleading and androgynous, Rollie it is.

Rollie with her mother
Bel Bacon Thorne c. 1920

William Dennis Marks
at the University of Pennsylvania
Portrait by Thomas Eakins 1886

My grandparents entered the New York–
Bermuda race of 1910 on the *Yo-Ho*, a motorboat
of Grandpa Bacon's design. Grandma was pilot.
They came in second; there were two entries!

Mabel Marks Bacon
c. 1910

My father was twenty and my mother just nineteen when they married—too young and too quickly, both their families agreed. They separated when I was three, and my mother took me to Pass Christian, Mississippi, a dozing, moss-hung vacation town on the Gulf of Mexico. Leaving me in the care of my grandparents, she moved to New Orleans to work a few months for the *New Orleans Item*. Later, in San Francisco, she was secretary to a novelist with whom she went to Tahiti. I visited her briefly in New Orleans and San Francisco but not in Tahiti, so I saw little of her until she returned to the family fold a few years later. My father stayed East. His forebears had been New Yorkers for generations.

My maternal grandparents, Henry Bacon and Mabel Marks, second cousins, were married when they were both very young. Their families also disapproved, partly because he had left Virginia Military Institute in his senior year to marry, partly because he was a "handful" and she was "headstrong."

Petite and pretty, Mabel Marks Bacon was one of two daughters of William Dennis Marks, Professor of Dynamical Engineering at the University of Pennsylvania. Her education didn't go beyond boarding school in Dresden, Germany, but her sister, Jeanette Marks, scholar of the family, became head of the English Department at Mount Holyoke College.

"Grandpa Marks," as we called him, died two years before I was born, but I grew up knowing that he was very much involved in the scientific and art worlds of Philadelphia. I knew that Thomas Edison, with whom he had a long, formal friendship, had hired him to design and run the Philadelphia Edison Electric Company. I also knew that my grandmother and her sister had inherited his portrait by Thomas Eakins and that, when hard times came, they sold it. Now it belongs to Washington University in St. Louis. What I didn't know until many years after I became serious about photography was that in 1888 my great-grandfather, collaborating with Mr. Eakins, had written the first chapter of *Animal Locomotion, the Muybridge Work at the University of Pennsylvania*.

One of thirteen children, Henry Bacon, a second generation Californian, was raised on a ranch in an area that later became the city of Pasadena. His father, Frank Bacon, was a moderately successful businessman and doting grandparent who indulged my mother by sending her money or buying her clothes when she was small. Nonetheless, he was reputed to have been a cantankerous father.

Despite parental doubts, my Bacon grandparents found happiness and adventure in their early married years. In Panama he worked as an engineer on the canal. During World War I, after earning his degree in marine engineering and naval architecture at the University of Glasgow, Scotland, he was in charge of the construction of submarines at the Portsmouth Naval Yard in Kittery, Maine. When the war was over, they moved to Mississippi and built a large clubhouse to accommodate their many friends who soon became paying guests.

For me, life in their sprawling lodge-style hostelry was never boring. Designed by Grandpa, it was filled with houseguests who stayed for weeks, my mother (occasionally), servants, cats, dogs, parrots and my uncles, Page and Bill. Page was ten years older than I, so we didn't play together. When I was about five, while my grandmother was in the hospital, I was told that she was going to bring me a surprise and, indeed, she did—the endearing companion of my childhood, Bill! The son of her middle age, he was more a younger brother than an uncle.

As we grew up, visiting children from the East and the Midwest splashed with us in the warm, shallow Gulf and smoked the miniature pipes we made from the acorns of giant live oaks. Most of the time we just "messed around."

By day the peacocks stalked and squawked in the yard, and at night frightening things happened. The colored nurse Lily Mae (one did not say "black"; "colored" or "Negro" was preferred) told chilling bedtime stories as guinea fowl, our sentries, screamed in the yard outside. One night lightning split the flagpole, a skinned pitch-pine tree, and sent it crashing through the roof into the next bedroom.

Grandpa Bacon taught us to swim, to use tools, to laugh and to whistle through our fingers. He also trained us to shoot and respect firearms, drilling us never to point a gun at anything unless we meant to kill. My love for sailing began when he skippered our schooner, *Yo-Ho,* named after an earlier motorboat. With a black hull and tanned sails, she was my imaginary pirate vessel as we beat to Ship Island far out in the Gulf or gunk-holed up a protected bayou.

Grandpa was the one who meted out punishment. When we were naughty he made us choose between a shingle on the bottom or a bamboo switch on the legs. I chose the bamboo. It was less embarrassing and more dramatic to show off the thin red welts.

The club burgeoned, but we soon outgrew it, so we moved nearby and developed a large hotel, The-Inn-By-The-Sea, from the ruins of a sawmill. My grandfather designed it in California Spanish style and trained men from the nearby village of De Lisle as builders. By the time I was nine I was learning with them, banging up my hands and bandaging theirs and mine, too.

Grandma Bacon was slim in those days, but I remember her best when she was round, her face brown and lined, her blue eyes assessing everything and everyone. Seldom demonstrative but with a strong feeling for family, she imprinted us with a sense of duty, loyalty and responsibility. As a teetotaling, canny businesswoman, she held the financial reins, which she liked to control as much as my grandfather liked to play.

Rollie and her uncle Bill Bacon
The-Inn-By-The-Sea  c. 1926

He was my pal and I was his protector.

Built like a T square, Grandpa took stairs two at a time and went down a ladder face out. He loved the ladies, liquor and laughter. And the ladies loved him.

Henry Douglas Bacon
c. 1910

Bel Bacon Generelly
Drawn by Paul Swan c. 1926

On rare occasions, our resident artist, Paul Swan, his body bronzed and oiled, clad in a white, fringed loincloth and a headband, performed "interpretive dances" before a tall candle while his daughter, Paula, her fawn-colored Great Dane beside her, plucked a golden harp. This entertainment took place in a large, covered patio rimmed by banana trees, philodendrons, palms and red-and-blue screeching macaws. The servants and I watched from the shadows, spellbound.

Roger Generelly
1923

Determined to make us as observant as Grandpa Marks had made her, Grandma would take us for Sunday drives and award a penny to the one who counted the most blue cars, the most cats or maybe the most red-berried yaupon bushes or blooming magnolia trees. She was an ardent gardener who taught us to identify native trees and wildflowers and to appreciate the value of compost. One Christmas we gave her a load of well-rotted cow manure. She couldn't have been more pleased.

After an absence of several years, Mother, her divorce final, rejoined the family and, soon after, in the patio of the inn, married a tall, good-looking man I had never seen, Roger Generelly from St. Louis. I wondered why he pronounced his name with a French accent. Then I learned that his father, Pierre, had died in Brazil before Roger was born. That made him even more glamorous. When I was nine, he taught me to "drive" while I sat on his lap and circled the inn's driveway. For ten years he was the father I hadn't had. I thought he was a god.

Music was a major source of entertainment in the upstairs living room where we played records on the windup Victrola: "Making Whoopee," "Five Foot Two, Eyes of Blue," "Tea for Two," "Marie." At night guests played bridge and mah-jongg or gathered around the piano to hear my new stepfather sing "If You Were the Only Girl in the World." I worshiped him.

Roger was made assistant manager, subordinate to my grandmother, but his charisma and her exactitude made for a rather sticky relationship, so he allied himself with Grandpa. Together they charmed the guests with lighthearted conviviality, sometimes vying to tell the most ribald stories in the least appropriate company, which occasionally included me.

Unsupervised except for sporadic checkups on our bathing and dressing habits, Bill and I were nevertheless expected to change before dinner: I from linen shorts with a button-on blouse and striped canvas belt to a dress (an admission that I was, after all, a girl) and he from a similar grubby outfit to a clean one. Otherwise, little differentiation was made between me and my uncles; male and female roles were merged. While our elders were dressing and drinking, we practiced pool in the lobby, becoming a threat to the skill of the guests. For pocket money we scavenged for coins in the crevices of stuffed chairs or shined shoes for the family.

In blackberry time Bill and I would sneak off and climb a steep embankment to the railroad tracks—strictly forbidden territory. I carried a big stick to ward off rattlesnakes, and he clutched a pail, mainly for show, since we'd eat most of the berries we picked. When we tired of picking, we'd put our ears to the tracks to listen for a train, then substitute a copper penny and quickly scramble down the slope to watch, breathless, as the locomotive thundered by, shaking our precarious hold. We half feared and half hoped it would turn over, but the only catastrophe was to our pennies.

On rainy days I read or worked on my stamp collection, pretending to go to Togo, Arabia, Italy, Japan and other exotic places. Books and stamps (which came with stamp-sized images of the flags and rulers of the world) were my small windows on life beyond The-Inn-By-The-Sea. One day I would record some of these countries with a camera.

In this earthly empyrean where Bill and I grew up, there was also family dissension; we witnessed injuries, illnesses and, once, when a guest had a heart attack, death.

We enchanted our visitors and were enchanted by them. The great, the near-great and the not-so-great trekked through our entrance gate, where two Chinese pottery elephants bade them welcome. We were hosts to people of all occupations—from industrialists, bankers and doctors to archaeologists, painters and silversmiths. And, too, there was just John Doe, accompanied by his bride, his wife of twenty years or maybe his mistress.

Many names and faces have stayed with me, and our lives have crossed and recrossed. But, most of all, I have kept up with Danny Jones, the son of St. Louis friends, who came back to the inn many times. Twenty-five years after we chased butterflies and I sang "Ramona" while he played the harmonica, Danny taught me to use a view camera and encouraged me to take my initial trip to Italy as a professional photographer.

The-Inn-By-The-Sea
Pass Christian, Mississippi 1928

The inn was Grandpa's creation, Grandma's charge and Bill's and my playground. Here we rode our balky ponies, swam, learned daring tricks on the elaborate jungle gym on the beach, played tennis and golfed on the nine-hole course or the miniature "Monkey Course" replete with my grandfather's fanciful sculptures, traps and hand-shaped cement berms and ha-has.

Rollie
c. 1928

*We,* Charles Lindbergh's account of his epic solo flight across the Atlantic in 1927, hooked me on biography and flying. Once a Navy amphibian landed in our waters. The pilot took me for a short hop above the inn. Oblivious to any danger, I leaned out of the cockpit and waved to everyone below while a sailor held my feet.

The idyll ended painfully and abruptly with the financial catastrophe of 1929. Inn, cars, boats, Bill's and my beloved ponies, even most of the family furniture went to the mortgage-holders. Left with four hundred dollars in cash, we found salvation in the form of *Carlotta,* a seventy-eight-foot schooner loaned to us by old friends. With all seven family members and two servants, we cruised for months up and down the Mississippi and Alabama coasts, trolling for dinner as we sailed.

Every so often we put in for provisions, to enable the men to borrow money or to look for work. Then one day a storm forced us to shelter on Dauphin Island, Alabama. All nine of us, wrapped in old army blankets and lined up like cigars in a wooden box, spent the night together on the picking table of a tin-roofed shrimp factory.

On the island, not long after, abandoned Fort Gaines and its World War I wooden outbuildings became home when Grandpa and Grandma Bacon leased it from the United States government. Five-sided, with bastions, a dried-up moat, a portcullis and a sally port, the fort, along with its "sister," Fort Morgan, had protected Mobile Bay from Yankee invasions during the Civil War. In the summer of 1864, Admiral David Farragut, defying both forts, is said to have shouted, "Damn the torpedoes, full speed ahead."

Because we couldn't afford to remodel the fort itself, we converted wooden outbuildings into family and guest quarters. After several months of preparations, we opened The-Sea-Fort-Inn—five dollars a day per couple, American Plan. A few adventurous guests from happier days at The-Inn-By-The-Sea began to arrive.

It was a scratchy life for our elders, but as far as Bill and I were concerned, we had found another playground. The island was heavily wooded with yellow pine, live oak and magnolia, the sand as soft and white as talcum powder. We cut palmettos the size of elephant ears, dragged them up the dunes, sat on them and war-whooped down. Exploring "alligator" holes in smelly, steamy ponds, we were chased by water moccasins. A generous friend had bought our ponies in Mississippi and shipped them to us. We rode like young centaurs on the hard-packed strand, dismounting when we saw sea-turtle tracks in the sand. If the eggs had hatched from their sun-warmed beds, we helped the baby turtles struggle to the sea.

Having cut our feet on them, we knew where the oyster beds were. We opened the shells and dared each other to eat the slimy things inside. One of our favorite games was a pitched battle with dried cow flops, bounty from cattle roaming at large. Digging for treasure, we found belt buckles, buttons and bones left from the bodies of Civil War soldiers. Lead bullets were almost as plentiful as sea shells, but our special trophy was a skull with a hole—a minié ball inside. Less dramatic were brass keys, shards of patterned household china and bits of glass made purple by sun and salt air.

But school loomed darkly over our halcyon days. At Pass Christian our one-room schoolhouse had been presided over by a six-foot maiden lady, Miss Nannie Sutter from California, who backed up her authority with a long, blue ruler, no less efficient for being painted with yellow-and-white daisies. We feared her but loved her, too, because she let us out to watch the rare airplane overhead. Every time I saw one I wondered if my father could be flying it. During recesses we played jacks, hopscotch, marbles and threw pecans from the schoolyard trees at one another, reenacting the Civil War.

Bill, and Rollie on Bill's pony, Bella
c. 1930

On Dauphin Island Bill and I had to walk a mile from the fort on a corduroy road to the village school. With three rooms and a teacher for each, it was larger than Miss Nannie's. It was also less friendly. Outsiders, we were fair game, and much of our time was spent squabbling with other children. A few weeks after classes began, Bill, small for his age, got into a fight. I flew to his rescue and, in the scuffle, threw his attacker down the schoolhouse steps. When the boy's mother, who lived next door, came after me brandishing an oyster knife, Bill and I fled home to the fort. I never went back. Two weeks later Bill's pony was found dead. A .22 rifle bullet had been inside her for days.

The rest of the family was also having difficulties. Under my grandmother's nose, Grandpa took a mistress and settled her in a house within the compound of the fort. Bill and I didn't know what a mistress was, but she couldn't have been good to cause Grandma so much pain and anger. Grandpa wasn't around much anymore. I worried then why my mother hadn't been with me when I was Bill's age. Did it mean she didn't want me? He and I were now closer than ever, but a seven-year-old boy and eleven-year-old girl have different fantasies. I longed for a friend or a sister to share my deepest secrets and a room I didn't have to give up to a last-minute guest. Mother and Roger, with whom I tended to side, quarreled frequently. There was no place for me except as a pawn in their unhappiness.

Guests, frequently stormbound on the island, came less and less often. We were barely holding our own. And there was still the matter of an education.

Just when our lives seemed in endless ebb, the tide turned. Roger found a job as assistant manager of the Pontchartrain, a hotel in New Orleans. As soon as we arrived I was accepted at Miss McGhee's, a fashionable day school for girls, most of whom talked about clothes, hair and boys—which seemed silly to me. I preferred assembling model airplanes of balsa wood and tissue-like paper. Few studies challenged me except ancient history and the making of a clay topographical map of the Tigris and Euphrates valley.

The confinement of our apartment made me miserable. I missed my buddy Bill and our old free-ranging life. Other girls had houses for their friends to visit, private dining rooms and, so I thought, happy families. Mother and Roger had hoped that they would get along better away from the bosom of the family, but their fighting only accelerated. Sometimes violent, it consumed us all in anxiety. When I was told that Roger had lost his job, I was glad. Now we could return to Dauphin Island, but, as it turned out, only for a few months.

# The South

The South is firmly in my soul. Although my parents were not Southerners, I was born and reared there. Not until I was in college did my allegiance begin to shift towards the East and my father's family. In 1954 I went back to Mississippi with John Malcolm Brinnin, the poet and biographer, on an assignment for *Mademoiselle.* I was in my element: clay and sandy soil, gravel roads, slash and loblolly pines, Spanish moss, white mansions, wooden shacks, black faces and warmth.

John and I went to see Eudora Welty and "her" country around Jackson. Although at first she resisted my lens, Eudora soon allowed me to photograph her. Gracious and forbearing, she took us to favorite spots she had photographed in the depression years. What was remarkable about the pictures we both took was how little the land, the faces and the architecture had changed since the mid-1930s. Much is still unchanged.

During my childhood, black people were an integral part of my daily life. When I was old enough to photograph them and they no longer took me for granted, I hoped that my pictures would reveal the sense of ease I had never lost.

If I had an intent, it was to show their dignity and self-respect in the midst of poverty. As Eudora Welty has said so eloquently, "My continuing passion would be not to point the finger in judgment but to part a curtain."

Bottles on the tips of tree branches are sometimes thought to keep evil spirits out of the house—perhaps as invocations of the dead.

Signs fascinate me. For years I have been searching for profound messages in those I see in the South: "Where Will You Spend Eternity?"—black lettering on a six-foot-square white board erected on the edge of a cemetery alongside a major highway; "Romeo"—the name of a Florida town with a cluster of wretched wooden shacks dominated by stinking smoke from a papermill; "C. R. Swindle, Farm Lands and City Property"—on a building in Mississippi. Sometimes it's born-again jargon, sometimes poignant juxtaposition, sometimes just funny coincidence. The real message is to keep on snapping and forget about semiotic profundity.

# Abroad and at Home
## 1932–1940

### *A Peripatetic Life*

Claude Schmit
1932

On my fourteenth birthday our landlady's son, Claude, quite unexpectedly, gave me an inscribed photograph of himself dressed as the Dauphin of France. On it he wrote, *"A ma camarade Rollie, C. Schmit."* He was nearly my age, and I was flattered to know that for months I'd had a secret admirer.

I N PASS CHRISTIAN and on Dauphin Island, I dealt with life from a relatively secure base, so when an opportunity came for my mother, Roger and me to go to Europe, I had misgivings, the strongest of which was leaving Bill. Yet I was ready for something new—even without him.

Our destination was Majorca, where Mother and Roger were to manage a hotel financed by acquaintances who'd been guests at The-Inn-By-The-Sea. But the deal fell through when we met them in Marseilles, so we went on to Paris, where we knew several still-well-to-do expatriates who might be helpful. In any case, we could manage to live there more cheaply than at home. For a few weeks, we stayed with friends at a grand house on the Rue des Vignes in Neuilly, then found a small place of our own on the Left Bank.

At the Alliance Française—its youngest student at age thirteen—I struggled with art, history and literature taught in French. The subjects were way over my head, but the language, forgotten today, came easily. A small group of English and American girls, several years my senior, adopted me and, after classes, took me to the Louvre, the Cluny or Le Petit Trianon. Afterwards, we rewarded ourselves for cultural endeavor by sitting outside at Le Dôme or La Coupole, where we gossiped about our fellow students or simply watched people go by.

Tension between my mother and Roger had eased a little since our miserable year in New Orleans, but I felt freer outside our apartment. After I had learned to use buses, I owned Paris. Happily neglected, I wandered the streets, absorbing as if by osmosis the plan of the city and the awesome buildings so unlike California Spanish, antebellum mansions or wooden shacks. I lingered in the Luxembourg Gardens, begging a chestnut or two from the vendors, admiring the statues—much grander than the fountainheads Grandpa Bacon had made— and watching with envy as French children sailed toy boats on the lake.

Bel and Roger Generelly
Rye Beach, New Hampshire
1933

In 1932, mired in the Great Depression, we three existed on a hundred dollars a month awarded Mother for my support. Our shaky financial situation really hit me one afternoon after school when I burst into the living room. I had just bought a pair of long-coveted china dogs with money saved by walking to school and wanted to show them off. Instead, I was told to sit down and be quiet. Mother, Roger and some friends were clustered around the radio listening as President Roosevelt announced a bank moratorium. The broadcast over, I was scolded. We could have eaten for days with money I had spent so frivolously.

To get us through the weeks until my child-support check could be cashed, we borrowed from friends and took on a piecework job, assembling hundreds of tiny book lamps called "Lampe Lido" on the dining room table for a merchant acquaintance.

As often as we were asked, we dined on Sundays with a family friend, "Aunt Fliggy," who lived at the Hôtel Lancaster in an elegant suite so tidy and formal I was afraid to sit on her Empire-style furniture. Despite her kindness, I thought she was a little odd. On her mantelpiece she had kept, for twenty years, an urn containing the ashes of her daughter Jean. Repelled yet drawn to it as if it were Aladdin's lamp, I fantasized that if I rubbed hard enough, something magical might happen.

Midway through our stay, my father, about to marry for the third time, came to see me. On a stroll in the Bois, he asked me to visit him in Connecticut. It was the fourth time I'd seen him. The first was in a New York hotel room where I slept in a Murphy bed, terrified that he'd close me up in it. The second was at The-Inn-By-The-Sea when Bill and I were quarantined with diphtheria; the third when I had shown him the stamp book I couldn't find when he left. After the Paris visit, I concluded, at least tentatively, that he wasn't really the bad guy my mother had been portraying for years. Maybe he had *not* stolen my stamps.

From the time we left Paris in the spring of 1933 until I entered junior college in 1935, we led a peripatetic life, including two years in New Hampshire during which my stepfather managed clubs in Rye Beach and Manchester before we moved to St. Louis. There he became a salesman for a wholesale grocery concern. Fortunately for me, a number of the parents of the girls and boys I ran around with had been guests at The-Inn-By-The-Sea. Even though we couldn't afford the schools their children attended, I was accepted.

The friendship of these fellow teenagers was heartening, but life at home was soul-shrinking. Under the strain, I fell sick. Fearing a recurrence of a childhood bout with tuberculosis, Mother and Roger sent me to Dauphin Island. When I returned, they said they were divorcing—half-expected news which now overwhelmed me. But, not too long afterwards, despair turned into acceptance.

After their breakup I enrolled at Gulf Park Junior College in Gulfport, Mississippi, just a few miles from my childhood haven in Pass Christian. I was relieved not to be living in the cross fire of an unhappy marriage, yet scared being on my own. Having shed one skin, I was awaiting another.

At Gulf Park I found a hockey field, tennis courts and a swimming pool. Ancient live oaks with long gray beards of Spanish moss were scattered among the California-style buildings reminiscent of The-Inn-By-The-Sea. Gray as the moss, the shallow Gulf of Mexico stretched towards infinity. Entranced to sight several small catboats tied up to a pier, I knew I was back again on familiar territory.

The girls at Gulf Park were friendly, but I confided my unhappiness over my parents' divorce only to my diary and, later, to a girl two years my senior. Helen Taggart would become my confidante and lifelong friend. My fears were soon substantiated by a telegram from Roger: *Your mother and I completely divorced today. Please be human to her, she needs your sympathy.* But the next day an unexpected antidote came from Grandfather Thorne saying that he was setting up a trust for me to complete my education. I had been earning my tuition with a small scholarship and by teaching tennis and sailing.

Without a home base, I spent vacations getting acquainted with the Thorne family in Connecticut and catching up with the Bacons in Fort Walton Beach, Florida. There Grandma Bacon and Page had started yet another inn, Bacons-By-The-Sea, the logistics of innkeeping on Dauphin Island having become too daunting. Although he visited Grandma often, Grandpa continued to live with his mistress. Other members of what I still thought of as my family were scattered. Bill was occupied with school. Mother was in Chicago and Roger in Greenville, Mississippi, each looking for a new spouse.

Welcoming me as warmly as if I were another daughter, Helen Taggart's mother and father became my surrogate parents for the summers I spent at their cottage on Higgins Lake, Michigan, sailing and palling around with Helen's sisters and their friends.

After two years at Gulf Park, I took pre-entrance examinations at Vassar College and was accepted. My tuition, room and board were paid by Grandfather Thorne. Child-support money and self-help work at a nearby greenhouse took care of the rest, allowing me to look the part of a Vassar girl in a skirt, matching sweater, pearls and clean saddle shoes. The truly chic among us wore Austrian shoes handmade by Peter Limmer in Boston. In cold weather, nothing but a Brooks Brothers polo coat would do.

Contrary to widespread notions, Vassar girls were neither all rich nor all radical. By the beginning of sophomore year, we had somehow arranged ourselves in groups of ten or so by a process of natural selection. Differing from Mary McCarthy's supposedly fictional friends in *The Group*, we stayed more in the middle of the road than in the societal or political fast lanes. I proudly considered myself a liberal—then not a pejorative word—signifying tolerance and openness.

With Helen Taggart
1936

For Gulf Park's cruise to Latin America, I wore my first outfit that wasn't a hand-me-down.

Jack Hulburd
c. 1938

Ready to marry Jack, I went to Hal Phyfe's studio in New York for an engagement photograph. The result was a technically beautiful studio portrait, but it wasn't me.

Portrait by Hal Phyfe
1938

During my second year at Gulf Park, I had fallen in love with Jack Hulburd, a Navy flyer stationed at Pensacola. Twenty-six, he was an attractive, gentle, pipe-smoking man; ready, he told me, for comfort and a family. I was seventeen. Despite our difference in age, I clung to the idea of marrying him until my second year at Vassar. Yet when the announcement of our engagement appeared in the *New York Times*, I knew what I had suspected for months: I was *not* ready for marriage, but my courage failed when I flew to Los Angeles to say this to Jack.

En route back to New York on September 3, 1939, our pilot announced that England had declared war on Germany. Some passengers gasped, some wept, some begged to send messages instantly. In my mind was the realization that Jack would be one of the first to see combat duty should the United States become embroiled. When he came to see me a few weeks later, I mustered the strength that had deserted me in Los Angeles. With guilt on my part and tears from us both, I broke our engagement.

Determined to finish college in three years, I plunged into study. Majoring in American history, I maintained high grades until my senior year. Then, inexplicably, I lost momentum and nearly flunked out. The watchword at Vassar was "Everything Correlates," but when I read the questions on my Comprehensive Examination, nothing seemed to relate. After failing it, I was little comforted by the fact that nine out of ten of us in the same field had done poorly. Absorbing this calamity (and no doubt aided by having had two history papers published in the *Vassar Journal of Undergraduate Studies*), I graduated with a respectable average, no wiser in my special discipline, but buoyed by Vassar's dictate that whatever I didn't know I could find out.

Through my college years Thorne relatives had grown increasingly important to me, especially my grandfather Victor Corse Thorne. Born in Florence, Italy, he was educated at Yale and became a physician. Upon the death of his brother Brinck, a famous Yale football hero, he gave up medicine and took a law degree at Columbia University in order to manage the family estate. Yet he continued to be known as Dr. Thorne.

Unlike Grandpa Bacon, Victor Thorne was a family man. His son by his first marriage was my father, and he had four other children by his second.

Grandfather was sandy haired, nearly six feet tall. He got up at six-thirty every weekday, took a cold bath, ate the same breakfast and went to his office at 120 Broadway at eight o'clock sharp. On Sundays he usually attended the Episcopal church. By the mid-forties, his servants had already been with him for a quarter of a century. Louis, the chauffeur, held a special place because his mother had been Grandfather's wet nurse.

His hobby was golf, his passion, Renaissance painting. For years he worked at establishing the provenance of a particular oil painting, *Madonna della Impannata*, as a product of Raphael. Doggedly, he hired expert after expert to authenticate it, but was told it was only of the *school* of Raphael.

One night at his apartment in New York, he woke me up long after I'd fallen asleep. Assuring me that nothing was the matter, he guided me through a dark hallway towards the living room and opened the door quickly saying, "Look, look at that!" The room was black except for a single spotlight on the *Madonna.* I expected a newly discovered stylistic revelation, but what I saw were colors so vibrant they appeared to have been freshly painted. He was testing a theory that when one's eyes are thoroughly rested, colors appear more intense.

My stays at Thornebrook in Greenwich with Grandfather and his children were pleasures. Harriet and Victoria, my newly discovered aunts, not much older than I, embraced me as a sister. Tory chose me as one of her bridesmaids, and Grandfather allowed me to snoop in his storybook-scary attic—sure signals I was found to be "acceptable." I never bore the brunt of his disapproval or his temper. About his painting he would talk for hours, but he never discussed his private life. What I learned came from other family members and friends.

Grandfather Thorne's first wife, Katherine Cecil Sanford, was the daughter of Samuel Sanford, a financier of the New Haven Railroad as well as an accomplished pianist, a collector of gemstones and a generous contributor to Yale. Kate, a dark-haired beauty who divided her time between New London (then the nucleus of a small, fashionable clique) and New York, remains an enigma.

Victor Thorne and Katherine Sanford were wed in 1896 at Schoonhoven, in Black Rock, Connecticut, the summer home of his parents. Gossip had it that before the ink was dry on their marriage license, Kate "went through" all the ushers. Be that as it may, she lost little time in abandoning her husband and their infant son, my father. She then married George Sheffield, their best man—and three men after him.

I never saw my notorious grandmother. A meeting was once arranged by her daughter Mary, but when I arrived on the appointed day at Kate's house in New London, Mary was the only one to receive me. Less than a year later, Kate died of pneumonia. A portrait by Robert Henri, now hanging in my living room, is an enduring if not happy reminder of her. When I look into her face, searching for some resemblance to my own, I ask in vain why that proud and handsome woman did not care to know her oldest grandchild.

Grandfather's graduation present to me was a check for five thousand dollars. With it I bought fourteen acres and a ramshackle house in Millbrook, New York, where other Thorne relatives had long been settled. To make it habitable I sought the help of a student at Yale University's School of Architecture. A mortgage assured the necessary repairs, and in a year it was ready to be occupied—a base, the beginning of long-sought security.

Victor Corse Thorne
c. 1940

Katherine Sanford Thorne
Portrait by Robert Henri c. 1898

# Harriet van Schoonhoven Thorne
## 1845–1926

For those who could afford it as a hobby as well as for those who pursued it as a living, photography was the rage by the end of the nineteenth century. My Grandfather Thorne's mother, Harriet van Schoonhoven Thorne, became a member of the New York Camera Club when it was incorporated in 1888. It was the same year that Grandpa Marks had published his essay on Eadweard Muybridge.

From the Schoonhoven guestbook
1898

At Harriet and Jonathan Thorne's summer home there was a combined studio and office separate from the house. Harriet and Jonathan "commuted" to it every weekday as if they were going to work in New York. Many houseguests recorded Harriet's ubiquitous photographic presence in words and drawings in the Schoonhoven guestbook.

The studio was packed with costumes, shawls, bird feathers, fans, beads and bric-a-brac she used to create effects, dragooning anyone she found interesting to pose for her. Sometimes she put herself in the picture, using a long, flexible cable release or directing a servant to snap the shutter. Other times she photographed strangers, the maid, houseguests, her sister, her husband or especially her grandchildren, who thought it great sport to wiggle just as she was about to shoot. (Exposures took a long time then, and they knew that a sudden movement would blur the image.)

Architecture fascinated her. She took, among other things, exteriors of public buildings in Manhattan and interiors of her own house in New York and at Schoonhoven.

At the Okeetee Club in Ridgeland, South Carolina, while the men in her family were hunting quail and wild turkey in the pinewoods and the women sewing or writing letters in the ladies' lounge, Harriet was photographing everyone, black or white. Her pictures of Negroes are particularly sensitive, revealing a two-way trust unusual in the circumstances.

When her husband died in 1920, Harriet closed her studio and directed her sons to dispose of its contents. She lived six years longer. In the early sixties, a cousin gave me two large wooden boxes which I put aside. In 1978, unable to take pictures myself because of a glaucoma operation, I opened them to find a treasure trove: a hundred and seventy negatives and seven autochromes—the earliest color pictures. Family members supplied identification for almost everything and gave me their own vintage prints to add to the collection. What a pity Harriet couldn't have seen her show at the Yale University Art Gallery in the spring of 1979!

Uncanny parallels, my pictures, shown on the right-hand pages following this one, were made (with the exception of the shower shot) before I had seen my great-grandmother's work.

When "Turkish Room Engaged, September 3, 1894" appeared in the Schoonhoven guestbook, everyone suspected something amorous was afoot.

Hattie, as she was known to her intimates, had two passions, photography and her husband, Jonathan. When he grew old, Uncle Jontie, as he was affectionately known, often took the sun outside Schoonhoven's front door.

The composition and the quality of the light in Hattie's picture reminded me of one I had taken in 1951 at the Baptistery in Siena.

The young fishing guide from the Bang Bang Club on Andros Island in the Bahamas, taken in 1960, might have been a reincarnation of the old man on the left from the Okeetee Club in South Carolina in 1900.

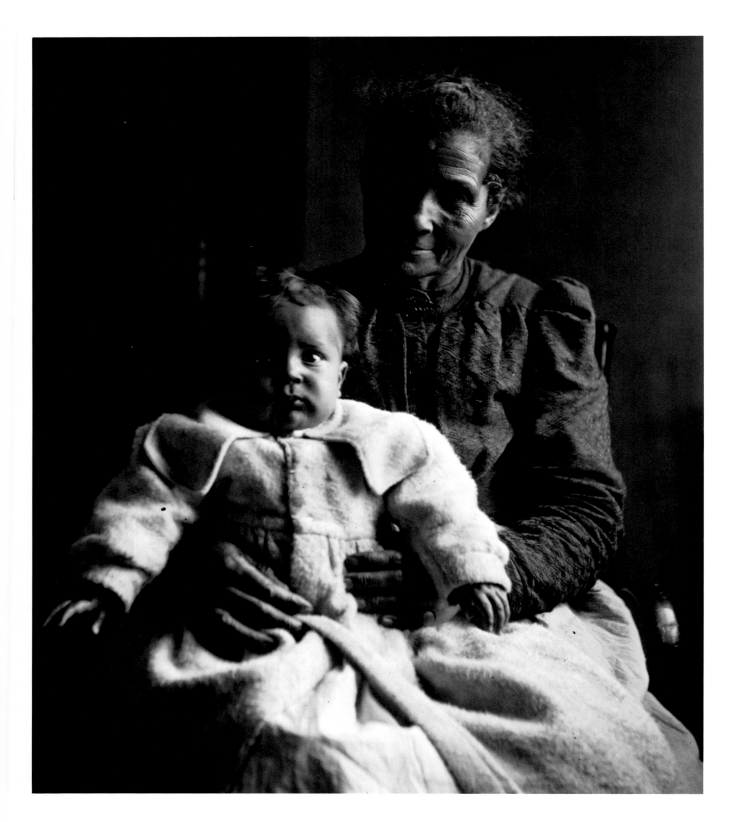

Mrs. Kitty Walker and baby in South Carolina, circa 1900, above, and an unidentified woman with two children in Mississippi, 1954—five souls, separated by half a century.

When we Thornes saw this picture, we had a good gossip about the identity of the man on the left—it was not Uncle Jontie! Then who? I know nothing about this daring deed ex- cept that the print was made from one of two slightly damaged glass plates. The friend I photographed in Key West in 1989 shall remain unidentified, too.

# Taos
# 1940

## *Thorne House*

A Penitente Cemetery
in Talpa, New Mexico

There was something mystical about much of the Southwest, a spiritual presence not necessarily kind, not overly threatening. It permeated the air, the sky, the desert and the people.

G RADUATED from Vassar, I drove to Taos, New Mexico, in the early summer of 1940 with my roommate Sibby Lamb and three classmates. It was my first trip to the Southwest, but I felt at home right away. Perhaps I was attracted to dark-skinned people and adobe buildings not unlike Grandpa Bacon's handcrafted architecture, or to the desert, so like the sea I had known all my life. We were planning to spend a week in Grandfather Thorne's large, hacienda-style house whose bizarre history I had not told my friends.

On the first morning, I got up before the others to explore the spacious, airy rooms of Thorne House. It had been freshly repainted, and its Southwestern furniture was handmade and new. The garden, far lusher than its neighbors', was surrounded by a high adobe wall. When I greeted the solitary Indian who was pretending to rake, he replied laconically, "You . . . granddaughter . . . Thorne." It wasn't a question. He knew who I was. Somewhat unnerved, I nonetheless attributed his prescience to local rather than preternatural knowledge. In Taos, word of *any* relative of Dr. Thorne would travel quickly. That night at dinner, I persuaded Grandfather's secretary, Helen Williams, to tell us how he had acquired the house from Arthur Manby, an eccentric Englishman who had moved to Taos at the turn of the century.

Arthur Rochford Manby
c. 1904

Her account is augmented here by recollections of family and friends and by published records:

*Arthur Manby had come from a good English family. He was educated, well-read, a lover of paintings and a fair artist himself. He may have been a remittance man, and many people called him a con man. Greedy for gold, land and the realization of his dream to develop Taos and his properties into a fashionable spa and resort, he was widely believed to have bilked many prospectors, murdered one (and probably four others) and swindled people out of vast tracts of land. The Taos Indians hated him, and he returned the feeling. His relationships with women were no more savory than the rest of his reputation.*

*In the summer of 1929 the state of New Mexico, from the governor down, was gripped by a gruesome discovery: Arthur Manby was found dead, his maggot-ridden torso in one room, and his head, its right side unrecognizable, in another. His dog Lobo was beside the body; another dog was tied up in a third room. A coroner's jury, hastily convened, accepted the local doctor's diagnosis that Manby had died of natural causes, and that Lobo, maddened by hunger and thirst, had chewed the head from the body. The remains were buried with minimal ceremony in the rear of Manby's property by the doctor and the few people close to him.*

*No sooner had the burial taken place than rumors began to spread. Why had nobody reported Manby's absence? Why had his house been unattended so long that it became foul with the stench of decomposing flesh—green bottle flies sticking to the insides of screens and windows? Why had his housekeeper, Teracita Ferguson, not reported strange doings? Was the body really Manby's? After the burial, several people claimed to have seen him in Mexico, in St. Louis, even in Florence, Italy.*

*Manby's brothers demanded that Governor Dillon of New Mexico order a thorough investigation, so the body and the head were exhumed and the internal organs sent to a pathology lab. The result of the inquiries proved murder, but the state made no official report. All that was revealed publicly appeared in the Taos newspapers; the head had been severed with a sharp instrument, the body shot through with bullets. The official findings have never come to light, and the murder remains unsolved.*

Grandfather Thorne had become aware of Manby about ten years before the murder. By chance, one of the conservators hired by Grandfather to authenticate his *Madonna della Impannata* had also worked for Manby. When he learned of this, Manby instigated what became a long correspondence. First, he offered to sell Grandfather his paintings and, later, used other lures to obtain money—vast land developments, a gold mine and mineral hot springs Manby claimed had a high radium content.

In 1921 Grandfather visited Manby in Taos, staying overnight at a hotel rather than in the house. He showed friendly interest in all that he saw and heard, volunteered no money but promised to have the hot springs' water assayed. Over the years, as Manby's fortunes began to sink lower and lower, Grandfather did make him a loan. Still, Manby became more desperate, "peculiar" and fearful. Living in one filthy room of his equally filthy house, he grew increasingly reclusive. When he was observed digging small holes in his garden and filling them, the neighbors assumed he was burying gold. At the height of his apparently paranoid behavior, Manby formed an organization he called the United States Secret and Civil Society, through which questionable deals, financial and otherwise, were channeled.

Thorne House in Taos, New Mexico
1940

Victor Thorne and his second wife, Clare,
photographed by
Harriet van Schoonhoven Thorne,
Victor's mother

c. 1910

Since Grandfather had practiced medicine for
years, one of his attractions to the Taos area was
the possibility of discovering radium for the
treatment of cancer. Clare died of the disease.

Grandfather and Manby's correspondence had gone on for nearly nine
years by 1929, and the maze of their dealings became too intricate to follow.
Suffice it to say that Grandfather, at Manby's death, held his paintings, his house,
the hot springs and a mine as collateral. But, not surprisingly, he found that
neither the hot springs nor the mine belonged to Manby. However, the house
and the paintings did become Grandfather's.

Obtaining clear title to the house, which had deteriorated in Manby's last
frenetic years, Grandfather sent Miss Williams to supervise its complete rebuild-
ing and refurbishing. When all was finished, he established the Taos Foundation,
which lent money to needy artists and gave money to the nearby Embudo
Hospital. Thorne House was opened for important local meetings. Artists were
particularly welcome. Physicians from the East were invited to spend vacations
there in exchange for a few professional hours given to the treatment of Indians
and Spanish Americans, mainly for tuberculosis and trachoma.

No one had seen the man who had spent so much money on the town and
the house. Why? Maybe, some residents reasoned, the corpse was not Manby's.
Perhaps Dr. Thorne was really Manby operating out of New York.

Mabel Dodge Luhan, queen of her salons in Florence and New York and
author of a mildly scandalous autobiography, knew Miss Williams. Like other
Taos residents, Mabel was doubtful of Dr. Thorne's true identity. One evening
Miss Williams took Grandfather to call on Mabel and her husband, Tony, a Taos
Indian, in their New York apartment. Since Grandfather neither looked nor
acted at all like the murder victim, Mabel was finally convinced that he was *not*
the disreputable Englishman.

After visiting Taos and hearing more about Manby, I understood why his
schemes could have intrigued Grandfather, but never have I figured out why he
chose not to set foot in his house. Certainly not because it was haunted. Mabel
may have laid the ghost of Arthur Manby to rest—at least it was not prowling
around when my classmates and I were there. We stayed on for another week in
the beautiful house with its bloody background before going our separate ways.

# The Southwest

Many times after Grandfather had acquired Thorne House I found excuses to visit the Southwest, photographing as often as possible, confining most landscape shots to color slides. Since superb photographers—Ansel Adams, Eliot Porter, Paul Strand, Edward Weston—had recorded the spectacular scenery beautifully, I limited my black-and-white shooting to buildings—like the old mission church in Nambé, Sagrado Corazón de Jesus—and to people.

Mary Lou Aswell and Agi Sims had been my tenants in New York before Mary Lou made Santa Fe her permanent home. As Fiction Editor of *Harper's Bazaar* in the forties and fifties, she discovered many gifted writers. Through her, I met the *Bazaar's* Art Director, Alexey Brodovitch, who bought several of my early pictures. She also helped me to reach the people in Taos and Santa Fe I most wanted to photograph.

Mary Lou was brilliant, witty, often depressed and genuinely camera shy. The only picture I took of her was at a party where, characteristically in basic black, she stood out—small, dark and magnetic.

Agi Sims—whose gifts encompassed painting, tapestry and pottery—lived next door with eleven dogs. She kept a protective eye on Mary Lou.

Willard "Spud" Johnson, a journalist of the Southwest, took me to photograph the Honorable Dorothy Brett, commonly called just Brett. Most often associated in Taos with D. H. Lawrence, his wife, Frieda, and Mabel Dodge Luhan, she outlived them all. Spud knew Brett, and his presence made photographing relaxing for us all. The first thing that greeted us was not her house, but the garage on which she and her Indian factotum had emblazoned her family coat of arms—six feet wide and four feet high! Brett had been deaf since an early age. The whitewashed walls of her studio were covered with her own paintings of Indians and people of uncertain origin, Indian artifacts and wires—wires leading from a wall clock, from light fixtures and from her hearing aid.

Mabel Dodge Luhan had rented a section of Thorne House in 1917 when it still belonged to Arthur Manby. Andrew Dasburg, the painter, had been her guest there. I was not aware of this when I photographed Mr. Dasburg in 1962, nor did he tell me, even knowing I was Dr. Thorne's grand-daughter. Manby's murder had taken place nearly thirty-five years earlier, but it was still not freely discussed.

The writer Winfield Townley Scott lived with his wife, Ellie, and their four children in an adobe house in Santa Fe. He was affable and outgoing, and the conditions for photographing were perfect, yet I had a hard time. I noticed that, despite his seeming ease, he alternately smoked and fondled his pipe, wrapped his arms around his chest or put his hand to his throat as if to reassure himself that he was still there. After many tries, inside and out, I suggested the egg chair. Perhaps it gave him protection.

Witter Bynner, the poet and translator, was just over seventy when I was in Santa Fe in 1962. On a brilliant day, he greeted me at the door of his rambling adobe house. A tall man with a slight paunch, his attire made him seem both debonair and formal. My eyes had barely adjusted to the darkness inside when I realized that he was almost blind and that the house was made gloomy by heavy Chinese furniture and open-work wooden screens covering the lower half of many windows.

He sat for a moment to catch his breath beneath an unobstructed window, and I made a few quick shots. From there, we went to his even darker, book-lined study, where he lit a fat, smelly cigar and sat patiently at his desk while I took several long exposures using a tripod like a monopod. Fortunately, the cigar had not survived the first puff.

My appointment book, Santa Fe, Tuesday, March 24, 1977: *To Laura Gilpin's. Bought a platinum print. Expensive but beautiful!* I have tried to make platinum prints and know how difficult it is.

In awe of her accomplishments as a photographer of the Southwestern landscape and of the Navahos, I had wanted for years to photograph her. She was not well, and I hesitated to ask her to pose. Then too, our styles were different, and I thought she might refuse.

She was a believer, as I am (particularly when photographing architecture), in the precise coverage of an entire negative—no cropping. Fast hand-held shooting makes such precision difficult.

As she sat in an armchair and I was confronted by her big, shining eyes and silver hair, I couldn't miss. She looked like someone's beloved grandmother. But when she went up to her view camera and picked up the cable release as if she were shooting me, *she* was the photographer in charge!

# The War Years
## 1940–1946

### *The Game Was Pressure*

In the Vassar Lab
1941

En route to the hospital, I questioned Dr. Bean about the life cycle of trichinae, and fantasized about little worms encysting themselves in my muscles, waiting for me to die so they could complete their life's mission.

AFTER I had broken up with Jack Hulburd, no wedding was on my immediate horizon. Most of my classmates married, but I had to support myself and pay the mortgage on the Millbrook house. Reared by the industrious Bacon family, I found work gratifying as well as essential. After six weeks of technical training, and later, a course in bacteriology, I became the sole medical technician in the pristine lab at the new Vassar College infirmary. Exciting at first, my duties became monotonous. The students were healthy, and nobody, except for a few diabetics and occasional sufferers from mononucleosis, had interesting urinalyses or blood counts—except me!

Waking up one day with aches in my muscles, especially the diaphragm, and having more lassitude than usual, I did a differential blood count on myself. To my dismay, I found an abnormal number of eosinophils—large leukocytes, or white cells. Consulting my bacteriology notes and lab manuals, I concluded that I had trichinosis. I had eaten pork roast a few nights before, taking care, I thought, that it was well done.

My boss, Dr. Achsa Bean, confirmed the diagnosis. Since she was driving to Columbia Presbyterian Hospital in New York for medical updating, she took me with her. After ten days of hospital bed rest, I recovered without aftereffects and went back to work. The boredom brought on by the "cure" made the Vassar infirmary lab seem like a first-run movie.

Still I was restless. For years I had secretly coveted a new kind of freedom. A desire to fly had been sleeping in me like a butterfly in a chrysalis ever since I had read Charles Lindbergh's *We*.

I learned to fly by the seat of my pants in a high-winged monoplane. Nothing has ever equalled my first solo. I felt at once infinitely powerful and frighteningly fragile. The sky might hold me forever, but the earth must receive me gently.

Throughout the summer and early fall of 1941, I was instructed in a Piper Cub J3 by a patient young man at a Poughkeepsie, New York, airport. But after ten hours of solo flight, I could no longer get fuel for joy flying. My wings were clipped, but my wish had been fulfilled. I considered training as a ferry pilot, but took no action. Employed at the Vassar infirmary lab for the academic year only, I had to look for another job.

On the recommendation of David Hulburd, an associate editor and the brother of my former fiancé, *Time* hired me in November 1941. For thirty dollars a week, I became, at first, the magazine's sole researcher in science and medicine. If ever I needed my Vassar training, it was then! Aware that I knew parlously little about either subject, I began to hang out at the magazine's morgue, pestering everyone who might answer my questions. At night, to further a fleeting and overambitious idea of becoming a doctor, I studied physics and chemistry at Columbia University, but soon gave up. A combination of duties at *Time* and the demands of city living stretched me taut; I was thankful to have my house in Millbrook for weekend retreats.

We were not at war yet, but most of the men I knew had already volunteered for one of the armed services. Many women had signed on as ambulance drivers for the Field Service, worked in factories, and took countless other jobs to free men for combat duty.

On December 7, with the bombing of Pearl Harbor, the war exploded in our backyard. Who born before 1935 or so does not remember that Sunday? Helen Taggart and her husband were visiting me in Millbrook. We had tuned in the radio for the symphony. Instead, we heard the announcement of what President Franklin Roosevelt called "a date which shall live in infamy."

The prospect of war left me in confusion, anger and fear for weeks. I plodded on at *Time* for six months, then quit. Financially a foolish decision, it was spiritually and emotionally essential.

Moving back to Millbrook, I recruited volunteers to plant a Victory Garden. Save one, all were women—"war orphans"—some from England, two from France. The sole man was 4F because of eye problems. We were all gung-ho about raising vegetables for the cause, and however motley, got along well.

After plowing up some of my land, we tackled a large plot donated by my elderly cousin Oakleigh Thorne on his nearby farm and sold our produce cheaply on the roadside and to local markets until fall. For several months after, I served as an airplane spotter, biding time until a more challenging opportunity would claim me and once more change my life.

During the summer of 1942, Congress created the WAVES—Women Accepted for Voluntary Emergency Service—"to expedite the war effort by releasing officers and men for duty at sea and their replacement by women in the shore establishments of the Navy." Educational institutions were canvassed; I was on Vassar's list of suitable candidates.

Three days before Christmas 1942, I reported to the U.S. Naval Reserve Midshipmen's School at Mount Holyoke College in Massachusetts. The pace was dizzying. No longer could I linger over coffee and a cigarette at breakfast or read for even ten minutes at bedtime. From reveille to taps, we were stuffed with facts from *The Bluejackets Manual*, bombarded with naval history, law, etiquette and dress codes, quizzed on the recognition of ships and aircraft. Inexorable drill and discipline exhausted me.

The game was *pressure*; whoever couldn't take it dropped out. Perhaps 75 percent of us stuck to it, emerging much as we had entered. But now we were ensigns in the U.S. Naval Reserve—WAVES. Soon, members of this dedicated group were stationed all over the American Area as administrators, cryptanalysts, teachers, physical education instructors or in any possible job that could relieve a man. When the gods were not smiling, we were drill and discipline officers. Such was my fate.

Daniel W. Jones
1940

I went out often with Danny Jones, my childhood friend from Pass Christian days, but he went into the Navy's V7 program to become one of the so-called 90-day wonders.

On the pistol range
1943

It was the custom for wounded flyers newly out of the hospital to spend several weeks in our office. They provided valuable and sometimes shocking information from combat areas. One lieutenant, who took Wednesday afternoons off to instruct officers and men in small-arms handling, suggested half in jest that I take over his class. "It's easy," he claimed. Enticed by the prospect of time off, I joined him on the shooting range. Thanks to my early training by Grandpa, I qualified as the Navy's first female expert pistol shot—by one point!

At the Naval Training Center in the Bronx, I became battalion commander with "supervision of company commanders and boots within the battalion"—of fourteen hundred women! No sooner had I reported than I began to connive for a transfer to a billet where I could live in a house, not a dormitory, and have regular working hours, not round-the-clock duty.

Most of my friends from Midshipmen's School were living in Washington. Every time I could wangle a twenty-four-hour leave, I went there to visit a WAVES friend and to sniff around for a transfer. One evening in the Roger Smith Hotel bar, a commander and a lieutenant at the next table started chatting with us. Commander Gyles Conrad, an old salt—judging from the tarnish on his braid—complained that he had been ordered to replace a male officer with a WAVES officer in the Bureau of Aeronautics. After another martini or two we exchanged vital information. I had no idea how to obtain a transfer, but the lieutenant said that he would "take care of everything." Following his instructions, I lied outlandishly, stating on the appropriate forms that my background had included several years of general association with aviation in addition to more than a year of flying experience. The spurious data passed uncontested through Navy channels. Receiving orders on April 7, I moved into a narrow, sparsely and unimaginatively furnished house on Thirty-third Street in Georgetown with three other WAVES and reported for duty the next day.

The Advanced Base Section in the Division of Maintenance of the Bureau of Aeronautics, with a complement of nine people, was responsible for compiling allowance lists of everything from underwear to aircraft engine parts for bases in the Atlantic and the Pacific. Civil servants typed the lists, attaching a federal standard stock number for identification. Other bureaus typed similar lists. Without benefit of a central organization, there was often duplication, omission, misidentification and misnumbering. Arctic clothing was sent to the tropics; cotton socks went to the Aleutians; engine parts were supplied for the wrong planes; too many jeeps and no personnel carriers went to big bases, and so on. My duty was to supervise the civilian typists, all women, who tended to resent WAVES officers. I then proofed and checked their lists with Chief Aviation Machinist Mate Thomas "Spud" Murphy, the unit's only technical expert. Spud and I got along like two potatoes in a patch on his boyhood farm in Indiana. He, too, felt that a gnat-sized system was being used for an elephantine undertaking. Fortunately, higher authority soon rectified the situation.

Commander Conrad was ordered by his superiors to send a technician and an officer to the Naval Supply Depot in Mechanicsburg, Pennsylvania, where an IBM procedure would compile and print allowance lists. He did not approve of this newfangled idea. But forced to comply, he sent Spud because of his skills, and me so that I wouldn't be underfoot. Women officers in general, and I specifically, were not to the Commander's liking.

At Mechanicsburg, the task of all bureaus was to give each item common nomenclature and a common stock number. The descriptions, with their numbers and quantity, were punched into IBM cards from which lists were made. Using the lists—a virtual wartime Sears Roebuck catalogue—the Navy's top planners could put components together to form different sizes and kinds of bases. Code names were assigned: a "Lion" was a large base, such as Nouméa; a "Cub" was smaller and an "Acorn," smaller still. Planners, purchasers, warehousemen, shippers and those checking goods at their destination then had identical lists.

The program, when finished and implemented, increased the efficiency of supply lines, saved money and, ultimately, many lives. The Navy awarded letters of commendation to all who had participated at Mechanicsburg, but Commander Conrad said nothing about mine. At that point I knew it was time to look for another berth.

My next one was educational but not challenging—Alternate Top Secret Control Officer to the Deputy Chief of Naval Operations for Air, Vice Admiral Aubrey W. Fitch. My immediate superior was his aide, Commander Russell Burke. In disseminating classified material to designated senior officers my acquaintance was widened, and I knew much of what the top brass was doing. But in reality I was a messenger, barred from discussing the information I was reading every day. Sometimes I had difficulty refusing papers to captains and admirals who were not on my distribution list, but I became skilled at dissembling.

My social life was at a stalemate, and work, however privileged, had grown routine, so I applied for shore duty in the Pacific Theater. My cousin Oakleigh L. Thorne, aide to Admiral Nimitz, Commander of the Pacific Fleet, wrote me saying: "I cannot understand anyone in their right mind wanting to leave the U.S.A." Nevertheless, he found a place for me. The transfer was granted and needed only my signature. I was torn. In going, I would have to be away from home for three years.

While I was procrastinating, Lieutenant Henry Dickson McKenna telephoned and identified himself by saying that he had met me at my house in Millbrook. I couldn't recall him, but when we had dinner and reminisced, I remembered and was strongly attracted to this tall, good-looking man. Formerly a photo interpreter attached to General MacArthur's staff and recently returned from Australia, he was now on duty in Washington—*and* he was available. Previous architectural training at Yale had imbued him with the spare, spartan concepts of the Bauhaus I had come to admire in the course of remodeling my Millbrook house. Our relationship deepened, and I soon abandoned all thoughts of transferring to the Pacific.

Dickson and I were married, both of us in uniform, in St. James Episcopal Church in Georgetown. My father, now a Colonel in the Army Air Forces, and my mother, now Mrs. Franklin Pope of Chicago, came to the ceremony. I was apprehensive, but everything went smoothly, though it was the first time they had been together since my father's Paris visit twelve years before.

Henry Dickson McKenna and Rollie at
their wedding reception
April 27, 1945

An old-law tenement
on Eighty-eighth Street in New York
c. 1948

While Dickson drew up plans and did as much demolition as he could, my chief job, after working hours, was to scrape paint which had built up on the woodwork since the 1880s like the layers of a baklava. Keeping the downstairs duplex for ourselves, we decided to shock the neighbors by painting the exterior of the machine-made red brick a jet black. The trim, originally a dirty white, became the blue of a Tiffany gift box.

Not long after our marriage, I was alarmed to learn that a massive invasion of Japan's mainland was being organized for imminent deployment. If this occurred, Dickson would certainly be ordered to go—not a happy prospect for either of us.

At this point both Admiral Fitch and Commander Burke were transferred. But before they left they secured me another billet at Op. 30 C, also known as Joint Security Control, where my duties were similar but even more hush-hush. In no time I got wind that something truly big was afoot. On August 6, 1945, the *Enola Gay* dropped the atomic bomb, ending the war. Dickson was out of the Navy almost immediately, and I was kept on until early December, when I joined him in New York.

On Columbus Avenue he found a cheerless apartment which looked like the interior of an abandoned Amtrak station today, complete with buckled, bare wooden floors, chipped black-and-white tiles in the bathroom and cockroaches. We both adjusted to civilian life slowly. The building boom had not begun, and Dickson's job as a draftsman paid very little. I wanted to be in charge of my own time, to work on my own—at what I didn't know—but we needed money, and I was lucky enough to be hired again by Time Inc.

As a Newsfront Department researcher at *Life,* I occasionally went on assignments with photographers. I was too inexperienced to draw topflighters like Alfred Eisenstaedt or Dmitri Kessel. Green researchers, especially women, were low on the totem pole and never on the masthead. In contrast, *Life's* photographers were treated with deference by their employers, not as necessary nuisances. Subconsciously I stored this revelation for future use.

When our dreary apartment began to depress us both, we borrowed money and bought an old-law tenement, illegally occupied for years, on Eighty-eighth Street in Yorkville, the German section of New York. Before we could touch the building, we had to persuade tenants to vacate, either by paying them off as handsomely as we could afford or by creating such havoc that they were eager to leave. As another unsavory task, Dickson had to learn whom in the building department to bribe for a permit to remodel. Our results, if not exactly International Style, were close enough for the architect Marcel Breuer to rent the top two floors as his first New York office and residence.

New York's postwar cultural life bloomed, and through Dickson I entered an exciting sphere I had only read about. We moved in architectural, painting, sculpture and dance circles, going with Dickson's friends to see the Ballet Theatre troupe and joining after-performance parties with John Taras, Rosella Hightower and Nora Kaye, whose companion at the time was the playwright Arthur Laurents. We kept up with the gallery openings of our favorites—Mark Rothko, Franz Kline, Alexander Calder, Henry Moore—and became friends with Connie and Lajos Breuer, visiting them in their first New Canaan house of his design or joining them in New York for drinks with Hans Knoll, the furniture entrepreneur, and László Moholy-Nagy, the Hungarian artist and photographer. Our closest friends were Isaac Hocs, a Latvian painter who had been to Yale University's School of Architecture with Dickson, and his English friend Pamela Preston (who in a few years would be my traveling companion in Italy).

Despite happy times and mutual interests, Dickson and I were often at odds; a whirlpool, silent and invisible, was slowly dragging me down. Leaving the Navy, remodeling the house, working for *Life,* partying at night and coping with financial problems had begun to drain my energy.

Sometime in 1947 I became ill. Pains in my right side and lower abdomen, fatigue and chronic fever all led to varying diagnoses of appendicitis, allergic reaction to a noxious paint remover or an idiopathic condition—medicalese for "we don't know." An exploratory operation revealed nothing extraordinary but, since my surgeon was already on the scene, so to speak, he decided to remove my appendix. Dickson came to see me only once.

Whatever my trouble, I no longer was in pain. After a few days at Eighty-eighth Street, where Dickson and I seemed to be in constant collision, I went to recuperate at my house in Millbrook. No sooner had I settled in than I received a call saying that Grandfather Thorne had died suddenly. God must have put his seal of approval on him, for he had just taken communion at Christ Church in Greenwich, returned to his pew and leaned forward to pray. An observant nurse nearby noticed that he remained in that position when others stood. He had been struck with a cerebral hemorrhage while following the ritual he loved.

No other death, I felt then, would crumple me so completely. To my further upset, Dickson did not accompany me to Grandfather's funeral.

Marcel Lajos Breuer
c. 1946

Connie Breuer
c. 1946

# New York

In the early fifties, New York was less crowded, less hectic and less expensive. It was not unpolluted. Incinerators from thousands of apartment houses produced a gritty black soot that collected on window sills and floors. The noise level was high. I settled there in my house in Yorkville like a native, but wandered all over town and abroad taking pictures.

64

It would have been less frightening to photograph a sleazy dive on the street than to shoot Times Square, on the left, from a shaky platform under the *New York Times*'s moving sign, a hundred feet or so in the air. As the years went by Times Square changed little. But elsewhere in town, skyscrapers, like tree farms, seemed to mature overnight.

When I heard that the photographer Lisette Model was offering classes, I signed up for my first and only formal instruction. She was a remarkable woman, a master of candid shooting, but a tough teacher. I lasted two sessions without one word of encouragement, but continued to roam from the Battery to 125th Street, watching and snapping. If this be voyeurism, my conscience is not ruffled. I think of my photographs as transpositions of something most of us like to do—people watch.

Much of my early work was for educational institutions. Some was for general public relations, some for alumnae magazines. These pictures for the *Barnard Alumnae Magazine* are part of an essay about city life by the novelist Diana Chang. The following brief excerpt from her second novel, *A Woman of Thirty,* is in the voice of her protagonist Emily Merrick: "Years ago I thought that . . . alone, I would die, that alone I would not be me, held in the walls of my body. Alone, I would find myself floating down a deserted Sunday avenue like an old newspaper, will-less, discarded even by myself."

The winter wind from the East River blows hard and cold, but old men played *bocce* in any weather when the United Nations was young.

Frank Lloyd Wright's Guggenheim Museum in Manhattan opened to a curious and critical audience in 1959, but it was this photographer's delight.

# Vassar and Europe
## 1947–1948

### *The Right Track*

Professor Richard Krautheimer
c. 1950

A master of the English language, but never of its pronunciation, he delivered erudite lectures with unique grunts, dramatic linguistic stresses, arm gestures so eloquent that his audience was transported almost bodily to St. Peter's at the time of Pope Julius II, to Florence when Ghiberti was casting the doors of the Baptistery of the Duomo, or to Istanbul and the building of Haggia Sophia.

MY RECOVERY from abdominal surgery was slower than expected, probably because of grief over the loss of Grandfather, who had been my anchor to windward since I was sixteen.

Thanks to a small legacy from him, finances were less tight. I quit my job at *Life*, still not knowing what I would do, especially when I realized that emotional support would not be forthcoming from Dickson. A child again, unsure whether I belonged to anyone, or anyone to me, I gravitated more and more toward Vassar, only a twenty-minute drive away. There, intuitively, I found the answer to my dilemma.

At the suggestion of Agnes Rindge Claflin, head of the Vassar Art Department, and Richard Krautheimer, Professor of the History of Architecture, I decided to go for a master's degree in the history of art. The Art Department had no graduate program, but Agnes wangled special dispensation, and financed by the G.I. Bill, I began classes in the winter of 1948.

My mentor was Professor Krautheimer who, along with a handful of other renowned German-Jewish scholars of art history, had emigrated to the United States in the early thirties. He was (and, at the age of ninety-five, still is) a mesmerizing speaker.

Dr. Krautheimer was short and dark with thinning hair and wild, bristly eyebrows. He was the most beautiful homely man I had ever known and certainly the brightest. His wife, Trude Hess, a scholar in her own right, worked with him hand in glove. Elizabeth Hird Pokorny, an architect who came weekly from New York, and Betty Meade, a resident landscape architect, completed my trio of teachers. Understandably, Dickson was unhappy about my going back to college and our being constantly apart, but I knew I was on the right track, even if I didn't know where it was heading.

73

Millbrook, New York
1948

I upgraded a mud hole to a full-fledged pond. To my disappointment, it never became a bucolic swimming hole, but remained murky and full of frogs, turtles, newts and leeches. Still, it was mine.

Studies were not so pressing that I didn't take time to enjoy what Grandfather Thorne had made possible: a house of my own and land. To provide upkeep for both, I leased the half of the house designed originally as a separate apartment and rented the fields to a neighboring farmer.

With help I planted hundreds of white pine seedlings given away by the government, started a small nursery of Japanese iris and raised standard black poodles. Dickson's two Siamese cats, my own hunchbacked, black-and-white kitten and a smooth-haired dachshund completed the menagerie. Wildlife of many kinds lived in the fields and woods around me. Baltimore orioles returned to their swinging nests in the big maple trees in front of the house, a happy omen soon to be tinged with sadness.

During spring vacation, I received word that Grandpa Bacon was dying in Pensacola, and I flew to see him. He greeted me weakly from his cot, this grandfather of my childhood, his nose beak-sharp in a sunken face as white as the sheet that covered him. There was no laughter. No off-color jokes. No ladies to flirt with. Just a once virile, charming man watching his life go out to sea.

Come fall, on a windy crystal day, I killed a cock pheasant in front of the Millbrook house in order to impress the men who were working on electric poles nearby. As they applauded my perfectly executed cross-shot, I bent to pick up my warm trophy. The breeze stirred his neck feathers—iridescent green, white and crimson. A tiny drop of wet blood stained his beak. Suddenly, suffused with shame and sorrow, I remembered Grandpa Bacon's admonition: never point a gun unless you intend to kill.

Now that I was thirty, the recognition of my own mortality came like a shot from the dark with the death of my two grandfathers. Simultaneously, I realized that the changes in my life were of my own making. This awareness was to grow stronger in the course of three years of analysis and the discovery of a profession almost predestined. But the initial insight came when they died and I reviewed their different paths. With the pastoral peace of Millbrook and the intellectual challenge of graduate work at Vassar, I began to take charge of myself. Solitude, which previously had depressed me, became a balm; studies, laborious in my undergraduate days, turned into impelling adventures.

I was ready for the change that would open my eyes wider than I had dared to hope. In late May 1948, after a semester at Vassar, I went to Europe to observe firsthand what I had studied. Dickson reluctantly approved of my trip, and my father gave me some money toward it. Reading my sporadic journal recently, I was astounded by how much I managed to do and see, and how clearly photography infiltrated my life.

I sailed from Manhattan on the *Parthia,* a small Cunarder headed for Liverpool. Making the most of a day's layover there before driving to London, I noted that

*not until you get close do you see there are no roofs. In London, I walked around St. Paul's which, possibly because of my classroom concentration on Gothic and Renaissance architecture, I find stolid, impressive, but a bit dull. The Cathedral is untouched by bombardments, but the area behind it is wiped out . . . St. Mary-le-Bow blitzed so only tower stands. Appalling.*

A day later I took in the National Gallery which, because of bomb damage, had only thirteen rooms open:

*Many pix cleaned. Some only partly to show difference. Rembrandts—cleaning reveals many objects in dark backgrounds, but still very much Rembrandts . . . Birdcage Walk, once fashionable houses, now grim looking government offices . . . Westminster Abbey ruined by the clutter.*

My education continued at the Victoria and Albert Museum, the Wallace Collection, the Tate Gallery, and the Courtauld.

Now three years past, the war had scarcely touched us as compared to Britain; food was scarce as well as rationed. Milk was for children only. Clothes allowed foreigners were denied to British subjects. Publically the traditional British stiff upper lip prevailed but, in intimate gatherings, the truth slipped out: *A middle-aged doctor said the other night, "We don't laugh very much nor sing, nor whistle."*

On June 14, I crossed the English Channel—Dover to Calais—on the *Invicta,* a veteran of Dieppe. The *Golden Arrow* crack train to Paris was waiting at dockside, despite the fact that Calais was still a rubble heap. Otherwise, France was a blaze of color. Every arable piece of land was used:

*Fields all planted to hay—being winnowed and stacked green. Wheat, potatoes and other vegetables, few cattle and not very fat. Exceedingly green, with brilliant rectangles of poppies, blue wildflowers and occasional bright yellow, like mustard. One wreck of a plane in a field. Lush country with poor looking people . . .*

I unpacked in a clean but dingy room in the small Hôtel Dagmar on Rue St.-Jacques in the student quarter and went out immediately: *People not shabby, food plentiful . . . music, warmth, life. Paris—so different from London. I began sightseeing in earnest: Ste. Chapelle, Notre-Dame, St. Severin . . .*

On June 17, I made a decision that was to guide the rest of my life: *Bought camera. Wanted one so badly, hope it's wise.*

Fontainebleu
1948

I took pictures of Chartres and Amiens, Fontainbleau and Versailles and, back in Paris, of Le Corbusier's Swiss Pavilion: *also Armée du Salut which rises like a ship on a dirty sea of buildings. It was in atrocious condition. The war and the spirit of the people have combined to drag the building down. . . . Ozenfant's house again, color frightful, dull pink with maroon trim.*

Pamela Preston
Venice 1948

She was tall, attractive and blonde. When men followed us in the streets, calling out "Guarda, che bella bionda!" she told them, with appropriate gestures, where they could go!

It was a Pontiac, a 35mm French camera with a good 50mm lens. By the end of the trip I had taken over a hundred shots of architecture and people. Some of the contacts and a few enlargements remain. Many negatives curled up like dried leaves because they were not kept properly in strips, but as individual frames. Luckily, most have survived undamaged.

I continued my coverage of "the city of light":

*Sitting on a bench near the Louvre, I was overpowered by luxurious use of space— ordered, clipped, on such scale that the gardens and plazas and the sky seem to be one. The Louvre was crowded and poorly lit and, after the National Gallery, the paintings all seemed yellowed.*

All the same, I looked until my eyes were blurred, my feet and back sore. In the evening I found just enough strength to join student friends of mixed nationalities, races, persuasions and tastes. At that time, Edith Piaf's "La Vie en Rose" was virtually an international anthem, but the craze of the young Europeans I partied with was American Negro jazz.

On my last night I went to see the city lighted up: *The Place de la Concorde was a great show; but too much light flattened Notre-Dame, making it look like a postcard. Moonlight or torch light, yes, but Mr. Edison, no.*

After a week of somber England, France had been welcome, but Italy struck me like a lightning bolt. Milan was not an electrifying city, but even there I found a faster pulse, a warmer heart: *I started my rounds as soon as the museums opened. Got into one tiny room of the Brera, otherwise closed until 1950–51 for repairs from war damage.* Still, a few of their choicest paintings were on display: Raphael's *Marriage of the Virgin*, Bellini's *Pietà*, Piero's *Virgin and Child.* I checked San Satiro, Santa Maria delle Grazie (*The Last Supper* was closed) and Sant' Ambrogio, which was under repair.

In Venice I was met by Pamela Preston, my friend from New York, who had married an Englishman whom she would join later. With Italian at her fingertips, a keen sense of fun and a yen for adventure, she made my trip. We went up the Campanile where, gazing down on the domes, the piazza with its buildings and sculptures and the Grand Canal, I imagined myself a character in a Canaletto painting. We plodded through the Byzantine section of the Accademia before reaching the splendid Tintorettos. After lunch we refreshed ourselves in the shallow Adriatic at the Lido. Two days more of art absorption and we were ready for the bus trip to Padua, Bologna, Ravenna, Rimini and San Marino.

After Venice, we found prices cheaper, the people poorer. Every town had its quota of unemployed hanging around the piazza. The women were mostly not to be seen. I remember astonishing resemblances between people on the street to those in the fourteenth-century Giotto frescoes we saw in Padua.

In Ravenna, we climbed up the scaffolding in the nave of Sant'Apollinare Nuovo to watch men replace the mosaics. That night I found a few tesserae in my pocket. After San Marino, whose chief revenue came from tourists and the sale of postage stamps, we boarded separate buses—Pamela for Positano and I for Naples (via Florence and Rome) where we planned to meet again.

Postwar political demonstrations and strikes in Florence, not to mention the invidious *turista* (diarrhea), kept me close to the Hotel Berchielli. Much of the city along the Arno had been destroyed but, enchanted, I knew I would return.

Still under the spell of Florence, I found Rome overpowering, but pressed on: Villa Borghese, the Colosseum, the Pantheon, the Capitoline Hill, the Forum. Whatever of Bernini's and Borromini's work I could find in the press of Rome's traffic, I examined.

After seeing Bramante's jammed-in Santa Maria della Pace, I dared question my professor's opinion:

John Cranko and Henry Leighton

*Cannot understand R. K's comment about its being a stage-set—no room for audience unless they hang out the windows. For kicks, I walked down to the Via Veneto and stared at all the Americans in the cafes, and come evening, wearily climbed the Spanish Steps to look at the full moon. I wonder what will come next.*

The inelegant Elti bus, filled with people, dogs and chickens in crates, took me from Rome to Naples: *We stopped at Terracina for ten minutes, a wretched town. Poverty south of Rome appalling. Nothing much left in Capua. Finally, Naples—where Pamela met me.* Her Positano house, buried in bougainvillea, was doubly welcome after a nerve-wracking trip on the torturous Amalfi drive. Plastered precariously to steep cliffs sloping to the Tyrrhenian, the village consists of white houses with flat shallow domes from the Saracen invasion.

Positano 1948

We swam all the next morning and were joined by John French, the fashion photographer, and two ballerinas from Sadler's Wells, John Cranko, the choreographer, and a friend of his, Henry Leighton: *Rejuvenated by our seaside dallying, we went to Naples which, as anyone can see is a dirty city, so full of beggars you can't move. We explored as much as we dared.*

Finding it impossible to sleep because of noise from the festas and saccharine Neapolitan tenors, we stayed up all night, admiring the moon and Vesuvius from our balcony and enjoying the din that at first had annoyed us. Until daylight the filth and the poverty were forgotten.

We went from Naples to Pompeii, with its haunting, solidified people and animals, its restored frescoes and roofless houses, its pornographic rooms, and then back to Positano. My journal trails off on July 29: *Days all run together.*

I gave myself over entirely to "La Vie en Rose."

# *Italy*
# 1948

My first trip to Italy could have come from e. e. cummings's poem "Memorabilia"—"marriageable nymphs" and "substantial dollarbringing virgins" invading Venice on a summer tour. Alike as omnivorous intruders, we differed conspicuously. Scarcely nymphs, I was playing hooky from my husband, and my traveling companion was marking time before settling in Kuwait with her new spouse.

After I bought the Pontiac camera in Paris, I was smitten with photographic fever. In my first architectural shots I was more concerned with effect than with accurate representation, as witnessed by this shadow of Michelangelo's eighteen-foot *David* in front of the Palazzo Vecchio in Florence, left.

In 1948 air pollution already had eroded the four ancient, huge, gilt bronze horses, part of which can be seen above, on the loggia of San Marco in Venice. The Torre dell'Orologio, or clock tower, dates from the fifteenth century.

Self-Portrait
1949

Self-portraits have never intrigued me. I took them, with indifferent results, only two or three times, whether from inability to accept how I looked or lack of interest in a set-up situation, I'm not sure.

# Vassar
# 1949

## *"Everything Correlates"*

RETURNING from three months of exploring the art treasures of Europe, I found, not unexpectedly, that Dickson and I had grown still further apart. He tried valiantly to share my enthusiasms, but could not.

Even my own country seemed alien, and the contrast between it and the war-devastated places I had just visited was unnerving. Cars were too big here, people too well dressed, stores too fancily stocked.

Savoring the exhilaration of the summer, eager to start studying, yet feeling guilty for putting my needs before Dickson's, I made the decision to live full-time in Millbrook, commute to Vassar and get down to work. Classes, as well as a design project and a thesis, were all-consuming. Even so, I was fascinated with what I was learning and thankful for distraction from private concerns.

For my architecture and landscape project, I chose to redesign a section of Poughkeepsie's waterfront from an oil storage depot to a public park with an Olympic-sized swimming pool, appropriate buildings and landscaping.

My thesis was a major undertaking. Professor Krautheimer had long been looking for someone to work up the history of Main Hall, the principal edifice of the college. Virtually nothing had been written about it, although its architect, James Renwick, Jr., already had many buildings to his credit, including St. Patrick's Cathedral in New York and the Smithsonian Institution in Washington.

Main Hall
Vassar College 1948

Mr. Vassar's "acre of consecrated bricks," modeled after the Tuileries in Paris and highly praised in its day, was a perfect choice for a master's thesis. The subject was right at hand.

Main Hall was a fine example of the mid-nineteenth-century eclectic architecture known as the Second Empire, or French style, after the architectural renaissance of Napoleon III. Some primary source material was kept in the college archives, and more original drawings and specifications turned up in the musty basement of Main Hall and in the College Superintendent's office. Dusting off long-forgotten records and searching my memory of American cultural history, I was well on my way to understanding what had eluded me as an undergraduate—"Everything Correlates."

When my thesis was nearly completed, I crammed for orals, squeaked through and planned to perfect my photography, with an eye to covering Renaissance architecture in Italy. It was really Professor Krautheimer's idea, and his encouragement came with it.

Meanwhile, separated by distance and confused emotions, Dickson and I had hung on another year, living by rote what little time we spent together. No particular episode precipitated our decision, but our marriage had eroded to a point at which divorce seemed the next sensible, though painful, step. For our failure we blamed ourselves and, at the same time, each other. The death of love came hard to me.

New York's laws made it difficult for partners to divorce on grounds only of incompatibility; Florida's did not. To avoid the not always valid, albeit quick and easy, divorce laws of Reno or Mexico, I began the six-month residency requirement in Fort Walton Beach. Before I went there, I acquired a Rolleiflex and a Linhof Teknika 4 × 5 view camera, and pressed Danny Jones, my childhood friend, to show me how to use them. He gave me Berenice Abbott's *The View Camera Made Simple*, which I kept in my gadget bag for handy reference. Staying with Grandma Bacon and my uncle Page at their inn, and grateful for the security they gave me, I learned the rudiments of developing and printing in Page's dank old darkroom—using instruction manuals and tips in the current photography magazines.

Waiting, I worked. Professor Krautheimer, writing from Poughkeepsie, agreed that several short trips to Italy rather than a single extended one would enable me to catch the light at different seasons and take stock of my progress as I went along. I would concentrate on Renaissance architecture, particularly the work of Brunelleschi, Alberti and Palladio. When I wasn't photographing or in Page's darkroom, in fantasy I was already in Italy, mapping out where I would go and what I would photograph. Finally, my decree was granted, and I headed joyously home to Millbrook to prepare for my forthcoming adventure.

Andreas Feininger, whose architectural photographs and book *Feininger on Photography* were an inspiration, showed me his studio in Manhattan which, by an ingenious arrangement of black-out blinds, could be converted in a trice to a darkroom. When I thought of my grubby, low-ceilinged cell behind the furnace in the Millbrook basement, I was determined to have, some day, a darkroom where I didn't feel like a troglodyte.

Many photographers were forthcoming with information and reassurance, but the Italian government, in majestic disregard of my pleas, was not. Richard (from this time on "Dr. Krautheimer" was dropped), who carried much clout in Italy because of his scholarship in both Renaissance and Early Christian architecture, had written the Soprintendenza dei Monumenti without effect, so I turned to the Italian Consul General in New York, who furnished me with a well-stamped, beribboned document that showed my serious intentions.

All my photographic equipment had to be preregistered days before departure—with lists in quadruplicate—sealed and held in customs until sailing. Since this was before X-ray examination of luggage, there was no concern about fogging the film I would have to declare.

Finally, on August 25, 1950, with a Minox camera from my father and, from other well-wishers, hugs, kisses and admonitions to keep my lens clean (or less polite warnings) I boarded the French Line's *Liberté*—a bit trepidatious, a bit proud. There was no reason why Dickson should have been there too, but I missed him.

Once I was reestablished in Millbrook, Danny Jones came for weekends to give me tips in the use of the view camera, critiques of my photographs and emotional support.

With Danny Jones
1949

# Vassar College

In 1965, long after "Female" was dropped from its title, Vassar College celebrated its centennial. Four years later, it went coeducational. Matthew Vassar, a wealthy brewer, had called it his "magnificent enterprise," referring to the concept of higher education for women, as well as to Main Hall. This picture, taken from Main, shows only a small number of the living graduates. In a hundred years, 26,282 women had matriculated.

88

A freshman, photographed for *Seventeen*, passing for the first time through Taylor Gate, left, was not as alone as she appears. A few feet farther and she will be engulfed by a greeting committee, shown to her room and have very few moments to herself for four years. Arriving dressed as ladies, students quickly shed heels, hats and stockings, put on shirts, jeans or shorts, shunned chairs for the floor and smoked up a storm.

Photographing Vassar some fifteen years after my undergraduate days was a nostalgic experience—outside seminars in spring near the "Libe" certainly took preference over surprise tests inside the classroom!

If the main subject is not photogenic, I look for something symbolic, something that will evoke or imply. The telescope in the college observatory was used by Maria Mitchell, an active feminist and America's first woman astronomer. In her poetic and passionate opening lecture, she spoke of the necessity for women to study the natural sciences. She said one day we might "travel from star to star . . . who can say that this power might not be ours in the next life."

Madame Laure
Paris 1950

In Paris I met a wonderful old lady, a Russian emigré who lived in a dark flat in the Palais Royal (not the Royal Palace!). She came complete with a parrot and two cats, too big a heart and too small a purse.

# Europe
# 1950

## *A Decent Beginning*

I WROTE a friend at home:

*The* Liberté *is an ugly, enormous floating hotel. With red neon lighting, rose colored drapes, gilt and lavish woodwork, it reminds me of an unhappy marriage between a night club and a Palm Beach furniture store—far from my favorite Bauhaus.* [A sailor myself, I also complained that there] *isn't any sensation of an ocean voyage—the sea is rough today but the ship is steady as old dobbin.*

I was more interested in *who* was on the ship, rather than *what*. After the customary boat drill and a chuckle over the French name for life jackets, *brassières de sauvetage*, I searched the passenger list for John Malcolm Brinnin, to whom I had a letter of introduction.

We like to say now that we had put off making connections until our last day at sea, lest we be stuck with each other. In truth, the second day out:

*I met Brinnin and had a good hour drinking and talking, which we will repeat tonight. He told me many fascinating things about a trip around the United States he had made with Henri Cartier-Bresson. Gala night we dined and danced until midnight, then went up to first class with the fancy characters until about three, when John folded.*

We haven't worried since about being bored with each other.

Don Perry on the *Liberté*
1950

On shipboard I ran into a young Harvard architect I had met the first day out. We joined a cabin class party and stayed up until five. By then, more jaded than sensible, we decided that we would meet later and drive to Italy.

*It has a sliding roof like a New York taxicab, and the best way to talk to [or photograph] anyone outside is to put your head through the opening.* Christened "Otsy": *it hots up, smells a bit on the steep climbs and roars down the other side.*

"Otsy" in Switzerland
1950

John disembarked at Plymouth to visit Dylan Thomas in Wales, and would later meet me in Venice. At Cherbourg I boarded a train to Paris, and—my French far worse than it had been at thirteen—at the Renault factory bought a small car, described in a letter home as: *grey, full of sass and jazz.*

Shipmate Don Perry, who had plans to work for an architectural firm in Italy, became *the ideal traveling companion—full of energy and ready to do anything, not on-the-make at all. No romance, just good company and mutual interest—architecture.* Unconvinced that we were not lovers, no innkeeper would rent us separate rooms.

Driving through France, we looked briefly at a few châteaux, stopped at Autun and the Romanesque church of the Madeleine at Vézelay. After a few more detours, we made straight for Switzerland at an average speed of about forty-five kilometers! Knowing that film would be hard to come by, I stocked up in Geneva, praying it wouldn't be confiscated at the Italian border: *my last* bête noire. Luckily, there was no inspection of luggage whatsoever and I breathed easier. We parted in Verona, and I began photographing.

Still without adequate passes to use large equipment for interiors, I wrote on September 15: *Today I received a lovely* permesso *to photograph, with the single exception that it reads* senza cavaletto, *which I take to be a tripod.* Fat chance of hand-holding a 4 × 5 view camera for a five-minute exposure! When I calmed down, I realized that in Italy nothing is done by the numbers unless they be counted in lire. What money couldn't buy, time, friendliness and dedication would. With these options, I stopped worrying about official papers.

Despite fatigue, the more I did the more I wanted to do: *I am much happier when I'm working. I can loaf easily when I have people around me, but when alone, I must accomplish something.* Since I was alone most of the time, I did a lot.

Taking advantage of everyone's goodwill, I cajoled other photographers I met through friends or the U.S. Information Service to do my processing or recommend a lab. Darkroom dealings were tricky, but there were welcome surprises. Writing from Venice: *I have found a man to do my developing here, through Dmitri Kessel* [I had met the celebrated *Life* photographer on the *Liberté*], *and he has developed eighteen rolls and several 4 × 5s. I saw the negatives, and he had done a good job. Fortunately, there were few lemons on my part.* But with another lab in Florence: *I've had such perfectly terrible luck with the guy who does my developing, and now a new one turns out to be no better. He has gone big shot, new car, etc., etc., and his darkroom is still filthy. When I complained about some dirt on a negative, he spat on his thumb and tried to rub it off!*

Venice was as exciting as it had been two years before, even more so because Richard and Trude were there: *I've found my spirits at much greater height since talking to Richard and showing him some of my negatives. Such a zeal for life he has. It's very infectious and beneficial to me.*

John Malcolm Brinnin had reached Venice, too. We met for breakfast, went to the Biennale and were joined by Truman Capote at Harry's Bar for lunch.

*Two martinis and a club sandwich—delicious but like no club sandwich at home. Well, the* enfant horrible *took an instant shine to yours truly because I reminded him of the girl in his first book,* Other Voices, Other Rooms. *Of course, I was flattered and put at my ease.*

After lunch, I photographed him and John together. The afternoon ended with an invitation from Truman for me to visit him in Taormina: *which I'll not do and he will forget.* I had mislabeled my film can and agonized over the outcome. But all went well: *The gnome looks dandy and so does JMB.*

Truman Capote
and John Malcolm Brinnin
Venice 1950

*Truman is tiny, a bare five feet, oddly proportioned, very* blond, *a good face. But a voice that sounds like a gnome's, high, squeaky, scratchy and very affected and effeminate. Withal, I enjoyed him and liked him—he's extremely bright, penetrating, witty.*

95

Angelo, sacristan of San Lorenzo, and his family 1950

Angelo gave me the run of San Lorenzo in Florence and, in exchange (although we never referred to it as such) I took pictures of him, his wife and their orphaned grand-daughter on the day of her first communion. When they posed in the soft light of the cloister so naturally, so simply that I caught my breath, I knew they were opening a door to their lives, not only to San Lorenzo. I shot this one straight, for it was all there before me and could be done no other way.

Even with Richard and Trude's support, I remained up and down. I was still having trouble with my Linhof and my self-esteem.

*September 19, 1950, Venice: I know now that I was a fool to try to do, with an inadequate amount of film, training and time, what experienced people have not been able to do before. Also, it's raining again today. Feeling really shot and desperate. I called Richard and asked whether he thought I should stay in northern Italy and redo these things I've been pecking at, or go to Florence and concentrate on a few things only until my film gives out and then get the hell home and learn something about photography before venturing on so costly and difficult a project.*

The following day I left for Florence, where things picked up.

My comfortable room at the Hotel Berchielli had a clear view of the Arno. Even in undependable weather, I covered more palazzi and churches in a week than I thought possible. Socially things picked up too. At the U.S. Information Service, I met Italians, Americans married to Italians, and was invited to their houses. The city was not too small, not too big. I loved it.

Since film that I had prepackaged for mailing from Millbrook had arrived, I could use the view camera for the Brunelleschi churches Santo Spirito and San Lorenzo. After unimpressive earlier results with interiors, I was eager to pass on some new theories: *Am becoming quite an expert on interior time exposures. First instruction: throw out your light meter! Most of my exposures vary now from two to four minutes at f22–32.*

Of all the buildings I covered in Florence, San Lorenzo remained my favorite. I did the nave, the transept, every corner, every detail, sometimes waiting for hours for the right light. It wasn't just the dignity, clarity and harmony of the architectural vocabulary, but the peace I felt there. Much of this came from the old man who was its custodian. He would take me anyplace in the building at any hour.

There was no question, even after relative success in Florence, that I would have to return to Europe in the spring: *not with despair as I felt in Venice, for I have accumulated a great deal of one sort or another—a decent beginning.* The rainy season was about to start. I set off for Rome to tie up the loose ends of my trip and myself into knots getting a visa for Iraq and a plane ticket to Basra.

Self-Portrait at the Berchielli
1950

The small hotels usually had bathrooms equipped with bidets: *The bidet is a wonderful invention—one can use it for its intended purpose and avoid baths for days, wash the feet, the laundry, and now, best of all possible uses, washing film. It is marvelously constructed for this purpose, having water jets coming in from all sides and an outlet—perfect supply of water which fortunately doesn't run too hot.*

Venice
1950

# Renaissance Architecture in Italy
## 1950–1951

"Cows are very fond of being photographed, and unlike architecture, don't move," wrote Oscar Wilde. While buildings like Alberti's Santa Maria Novella in Florence, below, don't move, things related to them do—people, animals, vehicles, shadows. Smoke and fog obscure them. Lack of sun can reduce their brilliance and minimize their texture.

I went to Italy to photograph Renaissance architecture as Brunelleschi, Alberti or Palladio might have commissioned me: to present their buildings faithfully and thoroughly. My photographs were not necessarily intended to be pretty or dramatic—they weren't postcards. My ambition was to sell the pictures as slides and study prints to schools and colleges that taught art history or architecture.

I had no assistant in Florence. Climbing the steep steps of the Campanile (Giotto's tower) with a heavy leather case over my shoulder, a tripod in one hand and steadying myself with the other, I reached a spot where I could shoot towards the Duomo, right, despite being interrupted constantly by someone wishing to pass. The small aedicula was designed by Brunelleschi. The magnificent dome with lantern, above (the dome itself a marvel of Renaissance engineering), soared just above the oculus. It was Brunelleschi's masterpiece, although the sculptor Ghiberti claimed some of the credit.

It wasn't easy to photograph in an Italian city. In addition to coping with capricious weather, I put up with traffic, curious adults who passed in front of the camera to see what was being photographed and mischievous *ragazzi* who delighted in annoying a street photographer—"Take my picture, lady," they pleaded. If I did, suddenly they were swarming all over me. If I didn't, as soon as I disappeared under the black cloth, so would a piece of my equipment.

It took time and preparation to set up for the right angle, and, occasionally, if I put off photographing too long, something blocked the light or the subject—in Italy, most likely a banner announcing an art show or a festival (in São Paulo or Manhattan it could be an entire building!).

Getting the right view, without distortion and with important elements included, sometimes meant violating someone's right to pass. Once, in Mantua, I noted:

*I've come to the conclusion that one has to be pretty brassy to be a photographer, even of buildings. It bothers me very much to disturb people in churches, but they don't seem to mind, and one old lady sacristan at S. Andrea urged me to plant myself on somebody's tomb to get a picture of the inside of the dome.*

In Florence at San Lorenzo, an elegant classical treatment prevails. As in other churches, people were walking all about, but they didn't show up on the negative because the exposure was so long: *If it looked like someone was going to roost, I closed the shutter until he moved on and then continued the exposure. That's the reason we so seldom see people in interiors.*

Detail of the entrance door
of San Spirito in Florence
designed by Brunelleschi

Detail of the "Gates of Paradise"
at the Baptistery in Florence
designed by Ghiberti

In 1555 Palladio signed a contract with the brothers Nicolo and Alisio Fóscari to build a villa on the Brenta Canal, not far from Venice. It became popularly known as Villa Malcontenta after the blonde Francesca Fóscari who, for questionable behavior, was said to have been banished by her father from Venice to the country. But it also was called the "House of Pleasure." Devoted as it was to the celebration of the harvest, it's hard to believe that Francesca moped about spoiling the festivities. This photograph from the Brenta side, quite unlike the opposite façade, shows the villa in 1950. Since then it has been extensively restored.

Villa Rotonda, also known as Villa Capra, near Vicenza, designed allegedly for Palladio's own use, has four similar façades, each affording a sweeping view. The side shown is the main entrance at the end of a long road between two high brick walls. This building, as well as many others by or in imitation of Palladio, formed Thomas Jefferson's taste in remodeling Monticello and designing the library at the University of Virginia. Jefferson called it the Rotunda.

Whether in imaginary buildings like Ghiberti's from the Solomon panel of the "Gates of Paradise" at the Baptistery in Florence, above, or in real ones like Palladio's Basilica in Vicenza from the Piazza dell'Erbe side, on the facing page, Italians, especially, are inseparable from their architecture.

My problems with both Alberti's monumental Sant' Andrea in Mantua, left, and Palladio's Loggia del Capitano in Vicenza, below, were scale and parallax. From classroom to reality there was a big jump, and I was caught off-balance by the difference in size between what I had visualized and what I found. Whenever possible I included people, animals, automobiles, furniture—anything that was familiar and close to the building. Even with wide-angle lenses and the swings and tilts of a view camera, I couldn't get far enough away from some buildings to shoot without their looking as if they were falling backwards. But soon, with my most charming smiles and the Italians' warm hearts, I found my way into apartments or offices two or three floors up. From there, I could photograph a façade without tilting the entire camera.

One of the oldest palazzi on the Grand Canal in Venice, left, the Venetian Gothic Ca' d'Oro, as its name implies, was once gaudily gilded in addition to having been painted brightly with cinnabar red and ultramarine blue. Now it is the Franchetti Gallery.

After covering Palladio's San Giorgio Maggiore and San Francesco della Vigna, whose façade design he shared with Sansovino, I took whatever pleased my fancy. San Marco's domes, above, evoked the mystery of eastern lands, opulent rituals of a religion and an architecture strange to me. For this view, I went to the top of the Campanile, but there was no way to hold my Rolleiflex properly, so I poked it through a metal barricade and angled it as best I could.

I hired a boy to help me with photographing. We rented a *barca*—not as fancy as a gondola but stable—for the equivalent of forty-eight cents a day. Ettore was my porter, my guide and my bodyguard—he kept the *bambini* away from my gear.

*It was a marvelous way to get places, see things and take Rollei shots, then land and shoot with the Linhof which required a tripod. We stopped for lunch at a little trattoria and tied up just beneath our table so we could watch our things. He was a great help, and I now realize that one of the reasons I was so terribly worn out each day was from lugging heavy stuff around.*

# *Kuwait*
## 1950

*If anyone told me I'd spend my birthday in an Arabian desert hunting with hawks and thirty Beduins, I would have told him he was utterly mad! But that's where I've been for the past three days.*

This was written to a friend from a tent somewhere in the desert of Kuwait or Iraq, one stretch of sand looking like any other. To our hosts, however, there were great variations in the hundred or so miles we had covered, navigating without compass or markers of any kind. I had joined Pamela Preston and her husband, David Curtis, and we were the guests of Jaber and Sabah, two sons of the then ruling Sheik, and Ezzat Gaaffa, the Sheik's secretary. Through Pamela's interest in the Arabs and their language, we had been asked to join them—a rare invitation for women.

At four o'clock in the morning, we gathered at Dasman Palace (best described as Victorian Colonial) in Kuwait City, where we were jolted into wakefulness with three small cups of cardamom-flavored black coffee and a sight straight from the Middle Ages. In the assembly room were thirty or more men dressed in *dishdashas* and *kayffiahs*, the traditional long robes and flowing headdresses. Some were servants or slaves, as black as the coffee they were pouring; others, sitting on the floor, were falconers, the falcons hooded and their jesses attached to the leashes on the men's heavily gloved arms. Many were sheiks and functionaries who, like us, were sitting on benches that lined the room. Ezzat, at the right, said they were discussing local problems and politics. He, elegant in a putty-

colored *dishdasha* (which he confessed later that he'd had made at Abercrombie and Fitch), played host. Itching to photograph this scene, I sensed it would be inappropriate.

We were about to engage in the sport of kings, not on foot with salukis like the poor Beduins, but in old American touring cars souped-up to maximum efficiency and reupholstered with Oriental carpets. When dawn came, the Arabs, except for Ezzat, left to pray at the palace mosque, after which the six of us, divided among three cars, with two falconers and a driver, charged headlong into the cold gray desert, tops down, throttles to the floor. The rest of the contingent went in another direction to set up our camp.

Our chief prey was the lesser bustard, a large turkey-like bird called by the Arabs a *hubara*. When we came to a grassy place, the hawkers stood up in the back seat of the convertible, unhooded their falcons and made a "woat, woat, woat" noise followed by a high-pitched operatic laugh designed to frighten the *hubara* into flying:

*Clever bird that she is, she will hide in the shadow of a "tree," really a bush no higher than my knees, and revolve around it, keeping it between her and the falcon. We came right up to one and couldn't see her because, like all desert creatures, she is predominantly the color of the sand. But, if frightened by the noise of the hawkers, she will* *sometimes fly. The hawk sees her and away he goes, as much as a mile, and dives on her. She usually flies low, the better to conceal herself. Most times, the hawk kills the* hubara *before we can reach them. Occasionally, if the hawk misses, the hapless* hubara *is killed with a shotgun and, once in a while, she gets away. If the falcon makes a mistake or doesn't find a* hubara, *he sits on a "tree," the car comes by, and the hawker calls him. It is rare that a falcon is lost— a serious thing, because he is worth about a hundred bucks.*

*When the falcon subdues the* hubara, *the hawker slits her throat "In the name of Allah, the compassionate, the merciful" (or he cannot eat it) and lays the breast bare for the hawk to have a taste.*

Our second victims were gazelles:

*We got ours by chasing it with the cars and shooting it down with a 12 or 16 gauge shotgun. This sounds like the wretch hasn't much of a chance, and, with the powerful American convertibles these Arabs loved, he can eventually be tired out. But it's quite a feat to shoot one from a car going 60–70 mph.*

The gazelles outsmarted us several times by running across soft sand, hard enough for them, but not for our heavy cars. We got stuck often and shot only one. I cheered, silently.

Photographing from a fast-moving Buick was also a feat. Unskilled at such rapid shooting, I had a hard time simultaneously balancing and keeping my head from getting blown off. When I did get an opportunity, the results proved uninteresting—gray from lack of contrast because of the heavy dust we stirred up. Pictures taken in the camp, which appeared like a mirage in late afternoon, were much more satisfactory.

Camp was an elaborate affair. David shared a tent with Ezzat, I with Pamela. The men had considerately turned our tent in an opposite direction from theirs and erected for us, a few yards away, something special that had belonged to the late

ruler: a tiny canvas privy with a peaked roof.

*There is scant privacy in the desert, and the average Arab man cares little for it anyway . . . yet they don't pee standing up like a Westerner, but squat like a woman with their cloaks gathered about them. It is a very modest business.*

In addition to our sleeping tents, and Jabir and Subah's, there was a living-room tent for us "gentry," furnished with Oriental carpets and a portable radio. A cooking tent, a generator truck to provide electricity, a huge water truck and a general-purpose truck for transporting the tents and provisions made up the rest. In all we were about forty people, including sixteen hawkers and fifteen servants. We ate the *hubara,* dark meat which tasted like pheasant. The gazelle was much like venison. Both were surprisingly tender. Inevitably, the men killed many other desert creatures, such as jerboas (little kangaroo rats), rabbits, hares, sand grouse, wild hawks, foxes, a wolf, an eagle and a vulture with a wingspan of eight feet. After two days more of hunting, we sped home to David and Pamela's house in Ahmadi.

There, in the Kuwait Oil Company's town—more an army encampment than a civilian settlement—I spent the next week sleeping, reading and writing lengthy letters. There was little else to do except look at oil tankers and drilling operations.

Kuwait City, dusty from lack of paving, and the sirocco, or *kaus,* as it is called in Arabia, was a teeming metropolis compared to Ahmadi. In the fly-blown bazaar, old men were having their beards trimmed in the *al fresco* barber shop or smoking hubble-bubbles on the curbs. Young Kuwaiti men strolled through hand in hand, passing women, anonymous in black, who were selling spices, rice, coffee, dates and bags of god-knows-what. Their children, squatting beside them in the dirt,

showed signs of trachoma. Pandemonium was added to confusion when a shiny, pale yellow convertible, horn blaring, would push through the crowd, the driver usually a successful-looking middle-aged Arab in a red-and-white *kayffiah*—maybe a pearl merchant or one of many smugglers of gold bullion.

The Kuwaitis had allowed me to photograph freely. Although the women were camera shy, I took every advantage, using a Rolleiflex or the Leica III F I'd bought in the bazaar the day before the hunting trip. Impatient for photographs as exciting as my experience, I processed film in 80-degree murky water at the 100-degree lab of the Kuwait Oil Company, and was lucky to get what I did.

# Work
# 1951–1953

## *My Banner Year*

Detail from the "Gates of Paradise"
by Ghiberti

Italian customs did not allow exposed film to be mailed out of the country but it could be taken out. To develop it at home meant I couldn't correct mistakes on the spot, but anything was better than going through the darkroom disasters of the year before.

DESPITE my engrossment in Italian architecture and the thrill of the Arabian desert, Christmas at home in Millbrook and time to marshal my thoughts were welcome.

By now I was committed to photography, but would photography have me? Another trip to Europe in the spring of 1951 increased my skill and confidence, allowing me to check off my original list of Renaissance architecture and even to extend it. There was also the luxury of time for retakes and for making portraits, a development that had begun to intrigue me more and more. That visit was satisfying in other ways, too. Divorce was behind me, and I met new people with ease. At last I was sailing my own boat.

Based in Florence without a car, I either rented one, took a bus or cadged rides with newly made acquaintances and friends, including Marjorie Ferguson, head of the U.S. Information Service, and Franco Giusti, her Italian administrative assistant. Barbara Emo, an American married to an Italian, invited me to Palladio's Villa Emo, still owned by the family. I had photographed it the year before just as crops were being harvested. In Fiesole I took pictures of Newell Jenkins, the conductor, and attended one of his concerts. At a party I met the legendary Una, Lady Troubridge (in her sixties, sporting a well-worn sweater and pants), former lover of Radclyffe Hall, author of *The Well of Loneliness*.

The Krautheimers were also in Italy. Richard, now assured of my ability, commissioned me to photograph details chosen from the lower panels of Ghiberti's "Gates of Paradise" at the Baptistery in Florence. Made of gilded bronze, they could be shot only on overcast days. To prevent "hot spots" and secure uniform results, soft light was essential. It was a tedious undertaking in a crowded piazza, but the reproductions in Richard's definitive monograph, *Lorenzo Ghiberti*, were well worth my struggle.

David Wright
1951

In London, I began portrait-taking in earnest: poets for the Poetry Center in New York and other writers and artists. Each art had its own tight circle. For some individuals, I had secured introductions, but "Poetry Center" was the open sesame. In other cases, I was passed on by one person to another. Some notable refusals were Christopher Fry, Francis Bacon and Alice B. Toklas, who said the only thing she liked about herself was the top of her head!

Because I didn't work in a studio, the ambience was always different. George Barker sat on an old boiler in a bombed-out area. David Wright was perched on the edge of his bed, preparing a sandwich, his room illuminated by a naked light bulb. Kathleen Raine posed on the front steps of a handsome house; Anne Ridler in an armchair in her garden; Cecil Day Lewis was at his desk at Chatto & Windus, publishers.

These first portraits set my style. When willing, my subjects became partners in the process wherever I encountered them. Bob Kaufman, a poet, was in jail in San Francisco. Philip Larkin, in London, stood properly trench-coated before a great buddha outside the Victoria and Albert Museum. Thomas Kinsella stood in the rain under a black "brolly" on a Dublin street; Seamus Heaney in a cemetery near Belfast while his children cavorted among the tombstones. With some of my subjects, I remained an acquaintance; with others, I became a lifelong friend.

At home, the big task was to organize architectural photos. Vassar College bought many, both as study prints and slides. With a sampling of them, I drove south to see Grandma Bacon and Page and stopped on the way at the University of Virginia, Duke and many other institutions to peddle my wares.

Helped by Richard, Henry-Russell Hitchcock, Clarence Kennedy, John McAndrew and other architectural historians, I soon had a long list of potential clients. Next, I assembled and circulated a traveling exhibition called Three Renaissance Architects: Alberti, Brunelleschi and Palladio. With a short introduction by Richard, the show went to at least twenty-one schools and universities, after which it was bought by the American Federation of Art. My profit was modest, but my name was "exposed," and hundreds of students saw a bit more of the world.

It was my banner year for shows and publication. The photographs taken for the Poetry Center were displayed there in November at my first solo exhibition—a very exciting night for me. Danny Jones, who encouraged me from the beginning of my career, and Ruth Adams, an old college friend, then Publications Consultant for the U.S. Information Agency, helped put together an exhibition of portraits for Vassar. Through her, the State Department bought several pictures to create an exhibition, *Young American Poets*, for distribution in Europe, the Middle East and Japan.

*Vogue* did a feature story on poets, an event that warranted a glass of champagne and a journal notation: *Check from Vogue, $500 today. Photographed it. Harper's Bazaar* bought and published several photographs, but my first check went to the New York Traffic Department because I had parked too near a fire hydrant while collecting from the Art Director!

By the end of the year, I knew I couldn't pursue my career from Millbrook, much as I loved living in the country. Coincidentally, Danny, about to go abroad for an indefinite period, relinquished the apartment he had rented in my house on Eighty-eighth Street. Lock, stock and barrel, I moved to New York and put the Millbrook house up for rent.

Safeguarded by an able assistant to run my small business, I sailed for England on the *United States* on July 24, 1953, with plans for a story which John Brinnin had lined up with Cyrilly Abels, Editor in Chief of *Mademoiselle.* In September we went to Laugharne, Wales, to visit Caitlin and Dylan Thomas—his reputation as a lyric poet having reached the status of celebrity.

On a biting January day the year before, John had brought Dylan and his wife, Caitlin, to my house in Millbrook for a weekend—days that portended events beyond all sane predictions.

The Thomases' stay had been a strain, not because of Dylan's behavior—which, blessedly, was a model of self-restraint—but because Caitlin, when she wasn't sitting apart from John and me and our guests drawing cartoons of us all, monopolized the dinner conversation—mainly with deprecations of her husband. Dinner over, she resumed her silence and leafed through magazines. Since she was such a beautiful, serene-looking woman, this behavior was as unexpected as it was dismaying. Nevertheless, I liked her and was relieved to find next morning that she could also play the role of loving wife and appreciative guest. After our two days of zero-cold sightseeing and picture taking, I drove her and Dylan to New York and deposited them at the Hotel Earle.

In Laugharne, Caitlin, at first wary, soon warmed up to me. Since Dylan was away on a speaking tour, we tip-toed toward friendship, tentative at the beginning and, less than two months later—when she faced the horrors of Dylan's dying in New York—firm and trusting.

When Dylan returned with his right temple freshly gashed, his eyes red and puffy, we decided to postpone taking pictures until the wound had healed.

My second visit a few weeks later, this time with John, brought us all into greater intimacy. Dylan's mother put me up at her house, the Pelican; John stayed in the room of the Thomases' elder son, Llewelyn, at the Boat House. Dylan's and my relationship was uncomplicated, easy and gently humorous.

At Dylan Thomas's Boat House
Laugharne, Wales 1953

# Dylan Thomas

If the world was his public stage, Dylan's home in Laugharne, Carmarthenshire, was his workplace. Here he sobered down, physically and spiritually. He wrote in a tiny wooden shack perched precariously above the estuary of a river, where the big tides rhythmically form sweeping paisley-like patterns. Looking up from his desk, he could see Sir John's Hill, "Where the elegiac fisherbird stabs and paddles" and "the loft hawk calls, 'Come and be killed.'"

Inside his eyrie were an ancient iron stove, two chairs, a bookcase and two tables on which were books, old and new, bottles of dried ink, paper scraps and empty cigarette packets.

The walls were decorated with reproductions of Marianne Moore, Bruegel's *Dancing Villagers*, Giovanni di Paolo's *Miracle of St. Nicholas of Bari*, D. H. Lawrence and a photograph of mine of W. H. Auden. Above Dylan's writing table, Walt Whitman kept a watchful eye.

Although he enjoyed a pint or two at his favorite pub, Brown's Hotel, he didn't write while intoxicated. He composed in a spidery hand on plain paper, repeatedly working, working, reworking and polishing—sometimes a hundred drafts of a single poem.

Dylan's mother, Florence, was happiest when her granddaughter Aeron spent the night at the Pelican. Half a mile away, off Cliff Walk, was a "seashaken house on a breakneck of rocks," the Boat House, where Dylan lived with his wife and their three children.

Laugharne (pronounced "Larn"), a tiny village of perhaps five hundred people, three bars and billions of cockles, lies along the estuary of the River Taf.

When Aeron and Colm, the Thomases' younger son, were not playing on the rocks or the brown, sticky sand of the estuary, they often went walking with Caitlin in the sun-shot woods above the Boat House.

Dylan Thomas's career didn't truly take off until he "hit" the United States. Readings at the Poetry Center and tours throughout the country where—in his own words—he "boomed and fiddled while home was burning," all but devoured him. The money he made, so necessary to support his family, passed through his fingers like water. The praise, so addictive, was fleeting. Still, he wanted to read again to his vastly appreciative American audiences and, above all, to write the final ending to his play for voices, *Under Milk Wood.*

Frenetic reading tours, sycophant-laden parties and late-night bar-hopping exhausted him, and just an hour before rehearsing the actors for the first New York performance of *Under Milk Wood,* Dylan was in particularly bad shape. On arriving at the Poetry Center, he vomited, declared that he could not possibly go on and collapsed in the green room. After half an hour, he was shaken awake. Pulling himself together, he directed for an astonishing three hours, urging the actors over and over: "Love the words. Love the words!" I was so dumbfounded by his recovery that I almost forgot to shoot.

When the night of May 14, 1953, arrived, the theater was packed. The audience, silent at first, then tittering, finally exploded into laughter on realizing that this was no highbrow affair but a loving, ribald tribute to a village. Dylan took fifteen curtain calls as tears slipped down his face.

On our last day in Laugharne, John, Dylan and Caitlin were in troubled discussion about whether Dylan should go again to the United States. John, in a difficult position and ever aware of all the problems, spoke only when necessary. Caitlin, though sympathetic, felt that America spoiled Dylan and that both his poor health (brought on by heavy drinking) and his unfaithfulness to her must rule out his going.

The fall after John's and my visit to Laugharne, Dylan arrived in New York for what would be his last trip. His need had outweighed Caitlin's fears. Three weeks later, on November 9, in St. Vincent's Hospital, after four days in helpless darkness, he died of an "insult to the brain," probably brought

about by what he claimed was the downing of eighteen straight whiskeys. Caitlin, uncontrollably anguished during his coma, ran amok in the hospital and, forcibly restrained, was taken temporarily to a private sanatorium. Shortly after, with Dylan's body in the hold, she took him to England on the *United States* and from there to Laugharne, where a plain, white wooden cross marks his grave.

A few months after Dylan's death, *Mademoiselle* ran John's story, my photographs and, for a first in America, the whole of *Under Milk Wood.*

It is sad and ironic that Dylan's fame would turn on so tragic an end, and that my career would be accelerated by it.

In 1957 I arranged for a rendezvous with Caitlin in Laugharne. We hadn't seen each other since Dylan's death in New York four years before. Though she had written me earlier that she had tried to take her life, with characteristic strength she had willed herself back. When we went to Brown's, she sat where she always had, at a round table beneath an anonymous photograph of herself and Dylan in their "lamb white days." As we reminisced sadly, I thought not so much of the nightmare of Dylan's dying as of the frigid day at my home in Millbrook when he draped himself in an old wisteria vine and, hamming his way through many moods, slumped prophetically into despair.

# *Portraits*

Portrait-taking for me began as a conscious rebellion against the prettification of the human face as practiced by studio photographers. It was also what came most naturally to me. I enjoy the special effort of photographing my subjects where they live, work or choose to be, where they are in command, most at ease. My challenge is to reach inside myself to catch the essence of a person—or what I feel is *an* essence. There cannot be one definitive picture. Human beings, gems that we are, have many facets.

In the year 1951, taking portraits of literary personalities became, and continues to be, my primary photographic obses-sion. It was chiefly because of John Malcolm Brinnin's support and wide acquaintance among the literati that I became accepted in their world. At that time, John was the Director of the Poetry Center of the Young Men's–Young Women's Hebrew Association on Ninety-second Street and Lexington Avenue in New York, now simply the 92nd Street Y. In this capacity, he commissioned me to photograph poets and other writers who performed there. Later, John and his friend Bill Read invited me to photograph people they would select for their anthology, *The Modern Poets*.

Robert Graves, Truman Capote and Sir Herbert Read at the Poetry Center

August, 1951: *The other day, I did Elizabeth Bishop, a great poet, who is short and fat faced.* [I realized later that her face was swollen from medication.] *Since she is a very disturbed person and goes on periodic drunks, she has deep circles. She wanted to look like a sylph with a swan neck (of which she had zero!) and she wanted a picture for her publisher, too. e. e. cummings's wife and Breitenbach had both done her. She hated the results and tore up Mrs. c's, so I was plenty warned and plenty scared.*

*I took a series in her New York apartment, direct* [head on, without reflectors or props] *and talked like crazy—I have no idea what about. I was determined to get an* expression, *regardless of her desires, and I did. The pictures showed no neck and revealed no beauty but fitted a realistic idea she also had of herself—intelligence. It was like hitting the moon! I find this infinitely satisfactory—but enough!—get me started about photography and I'm off. It's my future—no mistake.*

Probably I fooled myself that she was satisfied by appearing intelligent, but she allowed the pictures to be used even though she may not have liked them.

In 1954 I photographed her and her surroundings for the second time—in Brazil, where, on a break from an assignment for the Museum of Modern Art, I spent a few days at her shared house in Petropolis. Elizabeth was happy, at ease and casually dressed. I liked some of the resulting pictures, and so did she, but about those of herself, she wrote:

*The ones of* me—*well, I don't know whether it was the cortisone or what* [she was asthmatic] *or whether I'm just plain unphotogenic—I really wasn't so fat then, but I certainly look it—although cheerful enough, and almost as intelligent as the toucan. It isn't your fault—I just can't face my looks, that's all.*

Our third photographic encounter was in 1969 at the studio of the painter Loren MacIver in Greenwich Village. I have no record of how she responded to the pictures taken then.

Elizabeth and I enjoyed each other, sharing the same college and many friends, and were in touch from our first encounter until her death in 1979. In all that time she could not come to grips with her own image, but she never gave up the possibility.

It was a sultry August day in 1951 when I drove from Millbrook to Brooklyn to photograph Marianne Moore in her fourth-floor apartment at 620 Cumberland Street. She greeted me at the elevator with elaborate attention, took as much of my equipment out of my hands as she could carry and insisted that, before we began to work, I must rest and have a cold drink. I accepted, but felt somewhat uncomfortable having a much older person so solicitous of me.

When she asked what she should wear and which room we should use, I told her the choice was hers. All I needed was a lot of daylight. She arranged herself on a high stool in the crowded living room before a large, handsome desk to her right and a bust of herself by Gaston Lachaise on her left. I made about twenty exposures.

After a break for lunch at her favorite tea room (she swiftly picked up the check) we continued, moving to a bedroom where she put on a black broad-brimmed hat and, holding a pair of gloves which appeared brand new, posed in front of a chest of drawers as tall as she was.

By the end of the afternoon, I had taken about sixty pictures. Surely, some would be good.

As I was packing, I noticed that she also was preparing to leave. Thinking she had an engagement in Manhattan, I asked if she would like a lift. Oh, no! She was going to *escort me* so that I wouldn't get lost! Arguing with her was useless. I left her at the subway at Bloomingdale's—a small, dauntless figure in a long gingham dress and Mary Janes who turned and waved when she reached the entrance.

A week or so later, quite pleased with my efforts, I sent her a set of contacts and several enlargements. She replied with a typewritten note and a crisp five-dollar bill for

*postage, envelope and so on.* [She disliked all the pictures.] *The one with the hat and gloves is beautifully taken—in fact I do not like to say destroy them, but the expressions seem to me forced. How I could overcome my dead patience, as though all must be suspended till we begin to live again, I don't know.*

While I was still licking my wounds, a letter arrived with a squashed gold earring and a handwritten note:

*I think this little filigree earring must be yours; since I have not had any visitors since you were here & so kindly generous to me with effort and film.*

I wasn't wearing earrings then.

Over time she agreed, or at least did not object, to having one of the pictures appear in *The Modern Poets.*

On the track of subjects for *The Modern Poets,* I found myself in London in 1961. John Betjeman (not yet Sir John), a poet and a passionate preservationist of Victorian architecture, threw himself enthusiastically into the game of being photographed. In John Brinnin's company, we walked about Smithfield Market, visited a small church and other landmarks, but no background inspired us. Suddenly, John, who'd learned that Mr. Betjeman had somehow come into possession of a morning coat once belonging to Henry James, made a suggestion. We returned to the flat, where Mr. Betjeman excused himself while I waited in the hall. In a wink, he opened the door—resplendent in a fifty-year-old costume that fitted him perfectly.

Tall, thin, almost furtive, the poet David Gascoyne was not comfortable in front of the camera. As if subconsciously, he placed a flower vase, a table, a chair between us. In order for him to face the daylight and me to be far away enough to shoot, I climbed onto a wall in the garden. As the camera clicked, I heard a familiar voice behind me call, "Rollie!" It was a college friend who lived in the opposite house. Somehow, this simple incident relaxed us both.

Dr. Edith Sitwell and her brother Sir Osbert stayed at the St. Regis Hotel in New York, where I sought them out one March day in 1953. Sir Osbert, shaky from Parkinson's disease, allowed me, with utmost grace, a few shots of himself. Dr. Sitwell, dressed in black and a sequined black wimple (which she called a hat), had just returned from one of her visits to Hollywood. I remember nothing she said except that she was glad to be back in New York. Worried about the abysmal lighting, I pushed the dim table lights as unobtrusively yet as near to her as I dared.

The resulting picture, a close crop from one of twelve half-figure shots, pleased her very much. She ordered many copies and told her agent it was her favorite. Later, after Dylan Thomas's death, which grieved her deeply, she wrote for pictures of him, adding,

*It was I who first made Dylan Thomas's fame for him, when he was a boy of twenty-two.*
*Yours faithfully, Edith Sitwell D. Litt. D. Litt. D. Litt.*

Soon she was able to call herself Dame Edith Sitwell.

Jean Garrigue, a poet, came to my house in Millbrook in 1952. I liked her immediately. The weather was inclement, so we went to my makeshift studio above the garage, where, hoping to put her at ease, I made a stiff Scotch and soda for her, bounced two floodlights off the white walls and fired away. The only "prop" was the wood stove before which she obligingly sat. *Vogue* published her picture, but I neither heard from nor saw her again.

Robert Frost's farm in Ripton, Vermont, was the perfect scene in which to take the "rustic bard," and he played the part—posing in a field while twirling a long walking stick, roughhousing with his dog and walking on a dirt road. Backing into bushes and trees he asked, "Will the leaves show?" "Don't you want them to?" I asked. "Yes, yes, I'd hoped they would!"

Nervous at the prospect, I had assumed that so distinguished a figure as T. S. Eliot would be difficult to photograph. To my relief, he was calm and courteous, content in his cozy office—a neat clutter of books and manuscripts—and appeared to be a man accustomed to having his image "struck." I sat in the deep reveal of the high window beside his desk, leaning far back as I snapped. He was concerned for my safety, but all went well through twelve quick shots, and I began to pack up. "Is that all?" he asked. "Really? Will you have a cup of tea?"

John wrote me later:

*Eliot* glowed *at his portrait and said it was the finest ever done of him. Usually, he feels his photographs make him seem "adolescent or senile," whereas yours make him look his age.*

I was lucky: that one roll could have been damaged in the developing process and I would have had no backup.

On a summer day in 1968, when I arrived at the tiny gondolier's house in Venice which Ezra Pound shared with Olga Rudge, he was in his nonspeaking period. As Olga was serving tea, she said: "Ezra, Mrs. McKenna is here to take your picture. Do you mind?" He nodded, and I saw my chances disappearing. "Ezra, do you mind *very* much?" she asked again. To my relief, he shook his head, and my spirits rose. We went upstairs. In absolute silence, he sat in a fan chair with his head down and his eyes shut. Disconcerted, yet very much moved, I said what was on my mind: "Mr. Pound, you have a beautiful face." "Nonsense," he said, lifting his head, opening his eyes and pointing to the floor below, "The beauty is down there!"

In *Images of Truth*, Glenway Wescott wrote of his friend Thornton Wilder:

*At the conclusion* [of a confidential story Mr. Wilder was telling] *he held his forefinger up straight and briefly pressed it to his lips. (A good photographer named Rollie McKenna has photographed him doing this.) It is the gesture of the patron saint of Czechoslovakia, St. John of Nepomuk, who was martyred for refusing to divulge the secrets of the confessional . . .*

I don't know where Mr. Wescott saw my picture (it was first published in March 1957 in *Esquire*), but my reaction was one of both gratitude and puzzlement. In retrospect, I recall noticing that when I photographed him at the Poetry Center in 1951, Mr. Wilder's gestures had more than a touch of the clergyman about them.

James Dickey, poet and novelist, had not yet published his novel *Deliverance* when I photographed him in Columbia, South Carolina. Fun to work with and unabashedly showing his many sides, he threw himself buoyantly into our photo session. Posing with his son Christopher, he strode out onto the pier on the lake in front of his house and caressed his guitar. Drawing a taut bow, he shot arrows into the heart of an archery target and charged through the "elephant" grass in his side yard as if he were hunting in India.

Derek and Margaret Walcott were at the Eugene O'Neill Memorial Theatre Center in Waterford, Connecticut, in the summer of 1969, where Derek produced his play *Dream on Monkey Mountain*. With friends, we shared the first moon landing at my house in Stonington and, after several years had passed, a surprise afternoon in New York when, walking on Fifth Avenue, I had an overwhelming premonition that I would see them in a few minutes. Not long after, they divorced, and we have been out of contact for years.

# Latin America
## 1954–1955

### *No Opportunity to Rest*

Henry-Russell Hitchcock
1954

He was a generous man of Churchillian drive—
expansive in body, mind and spirit.

JUST as I was beginning to be recognized as a photographer of artists and writers, an opportunity too tempting to resist came my way. The Museum of Modern Art asked me to accompany Henry-Russell Hitchcock, architectural historian and coiner of the term "International Style," on a photographing trip to Latin America. I had some misgivings. It would be an arduous undertaking: eleven countries in seven weeks. My companion would be a man I admired, knew only slightly and with whom I had never traveled. We had to "cover" the best modern architecture built since 1945.

Most pictures for the museum's planned exhibition were to be large format black and white. For these I would use the Linhof. I shot color only with a Stereo Realist camera. For personal use, though there was virtually no leisure time, I took the Leica I had bought in Kuwait and my trusty Rolleiflex.

We began in Mexico. One day, waiting out the clouds until the sun appeared, I set up to photograph the tile-covered façade of Juan O'Gorman's library at the University of Mexico. Russell had gone ahead to scout. After focusing, I emerged from under the black cloth, cable release in hand, eye on the sky. At the instant of exposure, Russell, who handled his bulk like a ballet dancer, came racing back toward me. "Rollie, Rollie," he shouted, "the sun's out!" When the film was developed, a few particulars of the library could be seen on the edges of the negative—Russell's blurred image filled the rest of the frame.

At night embassy cultural attachés and Latin American architects frequently entertained us, and since I had to photograph during every possible daylight moment, there was no opportunity to rest. Dinner generally began at ten in the evening. Neither much of a drinker nor an informed talker, I deferred to Russell, whose brilliant theories and opinions intrigued us all. But after five or six Scotches he became increasingly garrulous and had to be coaxed into going back to our hotel at two or three A.M.

Bullfight in Lima, Peru
1954

All that I had read or seen in films was true—the mystery of ritual, beauty of movement, contagious excitement as the crowd roared or booed. But in this drama there could be but one outcome.

I got up early and, because we had canvassed our objectives the day before, preferred to work on my own. No sooner had I begun breakfast than Russell would appear, red-eyed and voluble, clothes only slightly more rumpled than on the evening before, burning cigarette stub in hand. He ordered two black coffees, two eggs, ham and toast and, without skipping a bite, asked me to send cables, check our schedule and be extra sure that I did not lose our tickets. It dawned on me that my duties were not exclusively photographic.

We stopped briefly in Panama, then flew to Bogotá, where "Montezuma's revenge" laid me low. As a consequence, Russell had to acquire other photographers' work. The flight down the spine of the Andes from Bogotá to Lima, in a noisy propeller-driven plane, was long and spectacular. Our Rocky Mountains seemed like anthills.

In Lima longer than in any of the previous countries, but not long enough to go to Machu Picchu (which I doubt either of us would have survived), we were urged to see a bullfight. Russell wouldn't go without me, and I refused to go without a camera. Whether apprehensive that I might like the gory spectacle or be confirmed in my abhorrence I was not sure, but I wrote: *It was the only way I could get through the ordeal—to see it through a lens.*

Lima to Santiago was an even longer trip. The city offered us two small but handsome houses to photograph and not much else architecturally. By now I was yearning for home, but the trip was only beginning. Argentina was next. The Pan Am flight to Buenos Aires through passes in the Andes, so near snow peaks we might touch them, was terrifying. Poor, dear Russell sat speechless beside me, his body spilling over the narrow tourist seat, airsick, his face ashen.

Grateful to touch ground, we found Peronist Buenos Aires stultifying. Talking politics with Hardoy Ferrari, designer of the chair which became popular as the "butterfly chair," and other architects only in places where they felt secure, confirmed our dislike of Argentina's regime. In the Lancaster Hotel, from which we sent cables home, we had to swear that there was no code hidden in our messages. To add to my uneasiness, I couldn't lock my hotel room. There was not much stimulating new architecture in Buenos Aires anyway, so we went south to La Plata to spend a day photographing a house designed by Le Corbusier.

After a short stop in Montevideo, we reached Brazil and found the building boom we had been expecting. São Paulo was abuzz with commercial activity, but as I photographed, something seemed wrong—there was no earsplitting clang of metal on metal, no nerve-wracking drilling, no loud stammer of the riveter. The skyscrapers were being constructed of brick and ferroconcrete.

More "Latin" than São Paulo, the business center of Brazil, Rio de Janeiro's new buildings, with their curved plastic shapes and prominent use of color and tile, were a joy to photograph. The city, a study in contrasts of both architecture and people, was thriving.

We stayed at the vast Copacabana Palace, with its main façade on the wide beach where bathers of every hue lay thigh to thigh. The rear windows looked down on the most squalid shantytown I had ever seen—so appalling that I had no stomach to photograph it. As I eased gratefully into bed at night, the lives of the strangers just below me invaded my dreams.

We went all over the city—to its suburbs and sixty miles out to Petropolis, where there was much new building and where the poet Elizabeth Bishop lived. After working intensely in Rio for eight days, I was able to spend a weekend with her in the house she shared with Lota Macedo de Soares, an arresting, cultivated Brazilian woman who knew all the country's architects.

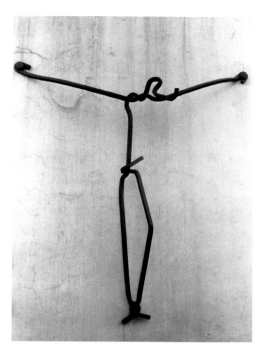

*Crucifix* by Mathais Goeritz
Mexico

When I had the chance, I shot something small or close-up with the Leica or the Rollei.

159

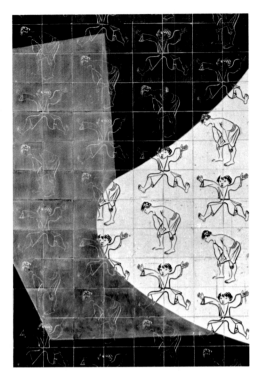

Tile Wall, Elementary School
Pedregulho, Rio de Janeiro
by Candido Portinari 1954

A few days more and we took off for Venezuela. If I was unhappy flying through mountains, it was because I had never spent fourteen hours over impenetrable jungle. Caracas came into view like Shangri-la.

Set amidst mountains rather than on the edge of an ocean, the city was flourishing. There was little new interesting domestic architecture in town, but skyscrapers of varying architectural styles were sprouting up like mushrooms from the soil of slum settlements. Since the new architecture was more International than Cariocan, we concentrated less on individual buildings than on masses of them. An exception was the Olympic Stadium of Carlos Raúl Villanueva at University City. A boldly cantilevered concrete shell formed a marquee over the grandstand, making the stadium look in side elevation like the open mouth of a giant prehistoric creature with the spectators' seats on the bottom forming even rows of teeth.

After brief stopovers in Puerto Rico and Cuba, we headed for New York. Exhausting as it had been—a round trip of about thirteen thousand miles—I felt privileged to have gone. I learned many lessons, the most important of which was that I found far less satisfaction in taking architecture in Latin America than I had in Italy. Primarily, I wasn't used to being supervised and rushed. Under those circumstances photographing had become a chore, not the pleasure it usually was.

With much fanfare, the Museum of Modern Art's exhibition *Latin American Architecture Since 1945* opened in December 1955. The black-and-whites, of which nearly half were mine, were shown in gigantic enlargements, and the color stereos, all mine, in individual stereo projectors. Unexpectedly, these images captured the reality of place far more accurately than did the big blow-ups. My photographs at the exhibition were supplemented by pictures of others. Credits were minimal, and my fight for recognition in publications that followed the show was part of an old story—the photographer's right to be known for his or her work. *Time,* reviewing the show prominently, gave pictures proper credit. *Art News* ran an article in which three of mine and a fourth by someone else were not credited at all. But my growing churlishness mellowed somewhat when in the *New York Times* Aline B. Saarinen said:

*Photographs, mostly specially taken by Rollie McKenna, are good, often spectacular. But it would have been hard to miss on that score, for in curves and color what Marilyn Monroe is to the Hollywood cameraman, Latin American buildings are to the architectural photographer.*

Henry-Russell Hitchcock was eighty-three when he died in 1987, leaving many publications and scores of friends all over the world. I count myself as one of them.

Caracas, Venezuela 1954

# *Latin American Architecture*
## 1954

The architecture of Brazil and Mexico was outstanding in the whirlwind trip which I made for the Museum of Modern Art. In Pedregulho, Rio de Janeiro, this elementary school designed by Affonso Eduardo Reidy is an essential part of a low-cost housing project. The school's classrooms are to the right, and to the left is a shell-vaulted gymnasium of ferroconcrete decorated with *azulejos* (tiles) by Candido Portinari of children at play. On the hill above, a sinuous block of apartments stands guard over the complex.

Another Cariocan complex, this one by the dean of Brazilian planners and architects, Lúcio Costa, is in Parque Guinle, Rio de Janeiro. It is called the Nova Cintra, Bristol and Nova Caledonia Apartment Houses. The many blocks of these buildings are not monotonous as such buildings often are. Mr. Costa had humanized and varied them within a unified design by using different colors, sun grilles and louvers. The outside stairwell adds a decorative as well as a practical fillip. Unlike most tiled and grilled buildings we saw, these, though already ten years old, were in excellent repair.

Oscar Niemeyer of Brazil designed this very personal, lyrical house, more curvaceous than the picture shows, for himself and his family in Gávea, Rio de Janeiro. It is cut into a hillside with a dramatic view of the ocean and a rock pinnacle. Rock is even allowed to enter the house at the level of the entryway. Nature's space and man's are one.

Max Cetto, the German-born and -trained architect, designed a house for himself in the seclusion of the Jardines del Pedregal, Mexico, where he practiced for many years. His home drafting room is special—lots of color, texture and a certain amount of playfulness.

When Cortés first came upon Tenochtitlán, the Great Temple of Mexico, he might have felt as I did when I saw this astounding sight. No human sacrifice, no hearts rolling down the steps, no thundering drums to propitiate Huitzilopochtli, the war god, but nonetheless, a shock! The Central Library of the National Autonomous University of Mexico was the creation of Juan O'Gorman, architect and painter. The façade, resembling a giant codex, is a mosaic of natural minerals of all colors, rich and soft. For all its strangeness, it seems to belong there.

# New York
# 1955–1957

## *A Babe in the Woods*

Edmund Wilson
*Esquire* Magazine 1968

By chance one day I opened a copy of *Esquire* and found inside a full-page portrait of the critic Edmund Wilson. Added to his clean-shaven face was a black moustache. My protestation to an editor was brushed aside: "No credit was given," he said, "What are you complaining about?" Subsequently, I spotted Mr. Wilson at a concert in Carnegie Hall. Expecting the worst, I went up to him to apologize. Looking puzzled, he said he hadn't seen the picture—the only time I was grateful *not* to have been given credit.

EVERY business has its own particular "beefs." Photographers seethe when they don't get credit where it counts, i.e., *with* the picture, not buried in a wasteland of tiny print in the back of a publication. We don't like credit given to someone else or our photographs copied. We holler to high heaven when our copyrights are ignored, our negatives borrowed, our prints held for months on end while editors make up their minds. When photographs are defaced or severely cropped without permission, we throw fits. When editors or art directors say they will give credit but make no mention of payment, we protest—resulting, more often than not, in the offer of a fee too low even to cover costs.

The *Saturday Review of Literature* showed a drawing of Dylan Thomas on its cover copied, without permission, from one of my well-publicized photographs of the poet directing *Under Milk Wood*. In the testy exchange that followed, I realized I'd get nowhere without suing—a process too costly for a neophyte freelance. This same portrait appeared in print twice many years later—with a credit not to me but to the Bettmann Archive. Today, most publications honor photographers' rights. But occasionally, in the press of deadlines, young staff members, not yet aware of what proper practice is, cause me grief.

When I first began to consider myself a professional, I was a babe in the woods of the New York marketplace. So, I joined the ASMP (American Society of Magazine Photographers), an unaffiliated union organized for the protection and education of photographers. It holds membership meetings, issues a monthly bulletin and puts out publications establishing codes of ethics, fair rates and acceptable practices.

Edmund Wilson
Wellfleet, Massachusetts 1957

### The Staff of the Museum of Modern Art 1960

Around the table from the left:
Porter A. McCray, Director of Circulating Exhibitions; William S. Lieberman, Curator of Prints and Drawings; Victor d'Amico, Director of Education; Peter Selz, Curator of Painting and Sculpture Exhibitions; Richard Griffith, Director of Film Library; René d'Harnoncourt, Director; Dorothy C. Miller, Curator; Alfred H. Barr, Jr., Founding Director; Arthur Drexler, Director of Architecture and Design; Monroe Wheeler, Director of Publications and Exhibitions and Edward Steichen, Director of Photography.

Drumming up business, photographing, traveling, keeping house, entertaining were time-consuming. As my activities broadened, I hired a part-time staff—a combination assistant-secretary-bookkeeper and, to help me in the darkroom, a technician. Most of the printing I did myself, because I loved it; but, subject to all the other pressures of a freelance, I found a first-rate in-house printer a godsend.

To quote a popular saying in the trade: "Every photographer needs a good old-fashioned wife!" With no wife but a dependable team behind me, I acquired two other clients whose assignments did much to expand my views and sharpen my technical skill—the Museum of Modern Art (MOMA) and the U.S. Information Agency (USIA).

Continuing to work for MOMA on an informal basis after my trip with Henry-Russell Hitchcock, I reported to Liz Shaw, Director of Publicity, for assignments: snapping celebrities at openings, doing occasional installation shots, covering the Education Department's art classes and other odd jobs.

One mid-April day in 1958, someone from the museum telephoned me at Eighty-eighth Street to come at once—it was on fire! I grabbed a loaded camera case kept on-the-ready and dashed downtown, worried about my friends there and about Seurat's *A Sunday Afternoon on the Island of La Grande Jatte,* which I had photographed for Liz not long before as it was moved into the museum in the dead of night. It was at MOMA on a one-time-only loan from the Art Institute of Chicago. The flames had calmed down by the time I arrived, but not the smoke and confusion. Hoses and water were everywhere. People were moving about like ghosts, trying to salvage art works in still-smoking rooms. It was a surreal and saddening prospect.

One man died and thirty-one people were injured. One of Monet's *Water Lilies* series, an eighteen-and-a-half-foot-long painting acquired by MOMA just three years previously, was destroyed, along with Candido Portinari's *Festival of St. John's Eve.* Eight other paintings were severely damaged, but the *Grande Jatte,* on the floor above the origin of the fire, escaped unhurt. The Art Institute allowed it to remain on exhibition for a second opening two weeks later.

By 1956, after I had done several pictures for the U.S. Information Agency, I was invited to become a contract photographer for their new Russian-language publication, *America Illustrated.* When Ruth Adams, who had been with *Life,* became Picture Editor of the new *America,* I signed up after a long, ludicrous security check. Dozens of my friends were interviewed, and an FBI man called on me at my studio. After I had filled in pages and pages of forms, solemnly sworn that I was not, nor ever had been, a member of any of two hundred and eighty-six organizations—from the Communist party to the Blue Star Mothers of America—I was fingerprinted by a detective of the Nineteenth Precinct and graciously allowed to continue what I already had been doing for more than a year. Nothing remotely secret ever crossed my bow in the six years I worked for the USIA.

Assignments that followed my clearance were as varied as fish in the sea: the United Nations during the Suez crisis; the New York Public Library; Leonard Bernstein; the interior of a Ford automobile; vending machines; the Worcester Art Museum and the National Gallery; the naturalist Edwin Way Teale and his wife; an exhibition at Pratt Institute in Brooklyn and a long picture essay on the Museum of Modern Art. I never knew what was coming next.

Fire at MOMA
April 15, 1958

The acrid smell, the sight of burned paintings and firemen hacking at charred walls is unforgettable.

Katherine Anne Porter
1956

When I phoned for an appointment, she asked that my pictures be "not too candid." Assuring her that I hoped to do justice to her famous good looks, she came back at me quickly: "At my age," she said, "one wants mercy, not justice."

The first literary person given me to cover was Katherine Anne Porter, for a story about Southern writers. As I wrote Ruth, October 8, 1956:

*I took her at her rented house in Southbury, Connecticut. She was very cooperative but quite difficult to photograph because she tensed up whenever the camera came near her; even though she is a good-looking woman. She insisted on making up her eyebrows and lips quite heavily, and the contrast with her very beautiful white hair and the skin of a middle-aged woman made for some incongruity. Her coloring is good and her eyes an unusual shade of something between green, violet and blue.*

She lived alone, surrounded by her French and Spanish antiques, and had just begun to work again on the novel *A Ship of Fools* which she had put aside for nearly fifteen years. A large cash advance from a new potential publisher had set her up handsomely.

The editors of *America* were enthusiastic. Miss Porter wrote:

*I am sorry about two things—that these proofs were kept from you for so long, and that I haven't the courage to choose any of them. It is painful enough to know that I have grown so hideous without having a print to remind me! You and your camera are not to blame—I am sure it is very fine photography!*

Eleanor Roosevelt
1961

Another legendary woman I photographed for *America* was Eleanor Roosevelt. She had two engagements on that day—as a guest at a Brandeis University class in Waltham, Massachusetts, and as a participant in a WGBH program, "Prospects of Mankind," in Boston. They left her revitalized and me exhausted!

# *America Illustrated*
## 1956–1962

In the late fifties an assignment for *America Illustrated*, nonpolitical and circulated in the Soviet Union, took me to Florida, where I covered the activities of retirees living on social security and pensions. I expected a relaxed, even boring, time being with people whose average age was probably over sixty-five. But I was in for a surprise. They were busy fishing, swimming, gardening, bowling, playing bridge, attending civic meetings and working part-time in local stores. Their children grown, their grandchildren occasional visitors, they had found time—as couples, as friends, as individuals—for happy community living. This assignment made such a lasting impression on me, I decided that as I aged, I would take pictures of others as they, too, grew older.

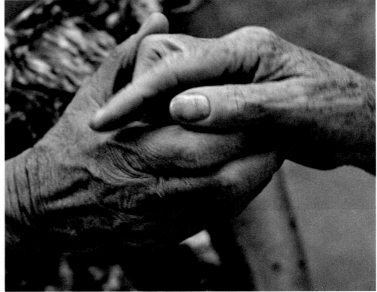

*America Illustrated* was the size and general format of *Life* without advertising. About half the articles were reprinted from leading American magazines. In exchange, the Soviets sent their version here in English. Ours was not a propaganda magazine, nor did it need to be to show that a large majority of Americans were better off than most Soviet citizens. Nothing I photographed was set-up, hyped-up or distorted. I portrayed what I saw.

Incidental to the main theme of a story, my photographs showed that most Americans had wristwatches, wore shoes in reasonable repair and smiled showing a set of well-cared-for teeth. Their houses had some modern electrical appliances and enough room for their occupants to move about with a modicum of comfort.

At *America,* in contrast to my earlier job as a researcher for *Life,* I knew I was appreciated. At least three other contract photographers worked there, all men. Assignments were given according to ability, not gender.

When asked to shoot a picture story of Helen Keller, who as a very young girl had overcome both blindness and deafness, I remembered my childhood resentment toward this paragon of virtue, constantly held up to me as a model of character. In ten minutes Miss Keller won me over—so moved by her at first, I was unable to photograph. When I did, I wondered if doing so might be taking advantage of her blindness.

Helen could speak in a monotone that, initially, I found

hard to follow. To "hear" my voice, she put her hand firmly on my face to get lip movements, throat vibrations and nasal sounds. Such intimate contact was disquieting, but in the warmth of her company I soon relaxed. We exchanged pleasantries and compliments easily and were on a first-name basis almost instantly.

I wrote to Ruth Adams in July 1956:

*Curiously enough, the clothes Miss Keller wore blended with the plants, flowers and trees, and her hands have the quality of wood and stone, working hands, well kept and strong, yet very gentle. The staring smile so often seen in pictures of her disappears when she becomes less conscious of strangers. Working in her study, she soon forgot my presence and went on reading Churchill's* World War II, *as if she were alone. Once, I touched her, for I thought she had fallen asleep, but she said, "Just thinking deeply."*

*I think she enjoyed the day, a glorious one. Just before I left she said, "It is wonderful to have pictures taken without tension." I hope these pix bear out her faith.*

From her extensive braille library in many languages, Helen could choose, among others, Zola, D'Annunzio, Conrad or Euripides. Books helped her, she said, *to build a world in which colors and sound took their place, even though I could not perceive them.* Before I left, she typed a gracious memento of my visit: *Lovely days like this one make my heart beat to a music no silence can destroy. It completes the glory of living.*

Helen Keller lived in Westport, Connecticut, in a Colonial-style house with her friend and companion Polly Thompson, who had succeeded her first mentor, Annie Sullivan. They talked volubly using a rapid hand alphabet. Asked to concentrate on her hands, I saw that they alone could not tell her story.

She wrote: *In the queenliness of the rose, the manifold shapes of young trees, bushes and grasses, I find eloquent witness to the glory that once trickled into the seeing hands of the Greek, the Japanese, and the South Sea Islander . . . On my walk by the cedar railing at home, I have noticed that the pine emits different scents—one wet with rain, one dry in mid-summer.*

Helen had an Alsatian as well as a dachshund. The pleasure she derived from petting and stroking her dogs was almost palpable. Once, as I was photographing her in the garden, a fly lit on her finger. Quickly, I checked myself from brushing it away. To her a fly was not abhorrent, but a welcome contact with another living creature. My editor wrote me about the reception of Miss Keller's picture story in the Soviet Union: *The magazine was not only distributed—all copies were sold out in half an hour. We're delighted.*

A quite different assignment for *America* was the National Bureau of Standards in Washington, D.C. A "watchdog" operation, it establishes standards for government purchases, incidentally benefiting general consumers. It also tests the quality and performance of products and conducts research and development.

In 1956 this high-voltage X-ray machine was used in research on treatment for deep-seated cancer and in setting standards used in industrial radiography. I shot it from a catwalk four stories up while in the same laboratory a siren wailed every eight minutes and ear-splitting lightning cracked from a high-voltage generator. It nearly deafened me.

In contrast, I could scarcely hear myself shouting to the scientists working in the "dead room" used to test speakers and other sound equipment. Walls, floor and ceiling were all similarly honey-combed with sound-absorbing material.

Light bulbs of all types were tested on racks and by other technical devices, but some required the keen eyes of a specialist.

When the assignment was over, I felt as if I'd spent the day in a Coney Island fun house.

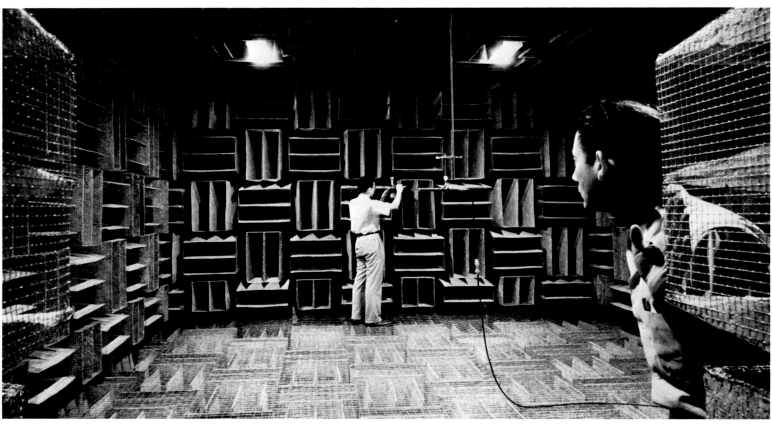

The Marlboro School of Music in Vermont in 1958 gave several concerts a summer and trained students in voice, piano, and wind and string instruments. What appears to be a heated confrontation between Rudolf Serkin and Alexander Schneider at a rehearsal break is but a friendly discussion of tempi or style.

Unlike the lively, open rehearsals, practice time for young musicians was calm, private and uninterrupted.

At Woods Hole, Massachusetts, Roman Vishniac, the photomicrobiologist, photographed the surface of the water and whatever showed beneath it with his Arriflex. Then he took a few drops in a petri dish to the nearby Oceanographic Institution where, through a microscope, he photographed in color and motion the organisms he had removed. When he finished, he returned every drop to the very spot he had found it. "Why should I break up their home life?" he might ask. "How would *you* feel?"

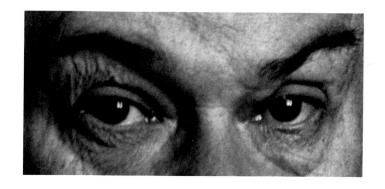

Before photographing in the woods near his country home, Dr. Vishniac would sit stone still for hours, if necessary, until his body absorbed the smell, the temperature, the "feel" of his surroundings. Small beings then knew he was trustworthy.

# The Museum of Modern Art

Throughout my New York years, the Museum of Modern Art was for me a mecca as well as a source of income: the photography exhibits were recurrent stimuli; like an old friend, the permanent collection was always there when I needed regeneration. When I desired a change, there were special shows—new photographers, new painters and sculptors, the latest in industrial and architectural design or a magnificent retrospective.

An oasis on tarmac—intimate, persistently inspiring—it was a unique gathering place. I felt comfortable there whether alone, with friends or entertaining out-of-town visitors.

In summer the popular cafeteria was open to the Abby Aldrich Rockefeller Sculpture Garden, where one could dine in the shade of a Maillol or a Moore. (The Junior Council chose this photograph of the Sculpture Garden for an "official" Christmas card in 1957.)

I had never seen a photograph of the painter Georgia O'Keeffe smiling, but the affable Director of the museum, René d'Harnoncourt, elicited one at just the right moment.

An exhibition opening is usually occasion for talking or drinking. Looking comes later. The Jackson Pollock show in 1958 was no exception.

Captain Edward Steichen, Director of Photography at the museum (and previously Chief of Navy Combat Photography in the Pacific), organized exhibitions which always captured the attention of the general public as well as professional picture takers. Here he is with photographer Richard Avedon and model Suzy Parker.

Children in art classes sponsored by the Education Department were far more exuberant and less self-conscious than adults.

In photographing Alfred H. Barr, Jr., Founding Director and guiding light of the museum, I wanted to do more than a head shot—hence the juxtaposition of Gaston Lachaise's buxom nude with Alfred's lanky frame and ascetic face.

# Henry
# 1959

## *The Evanescent Stranger of My Childhood*

Henry Sanford Thorne
c. 1954

Sustained by bridge, backgammon, golf, more-than-casual drinking and late-night revelry, he and his wife would fly back and forth with the seasons between New England, New York and their house on Nassau's Cable Beach.

I NEVER truly knew my father, Henry Thorne, until his final year, when his sixth wife had left him because he could no longer keep up the high-stepping life they had once enjoyed. Fun was their prime pursuit, yet they had clung to some age-old mores—among them, respect for the state of marriage. However fleeting a particular union might turn out to be, marriage in their social set was expected; living in sin was not. This pace exacted a price for which my father paid in hypertension, kidney dysfunction, heart disease—and the termination of as many marriages as those of Henry VIII. I was his only child.

As for my profession (which he thought of as a hobby), he couldn't understand why I made so little money. By 1958 I had gained a modest but solid reputation in a field in which he showed no interest—photojournalism centered in, but not confined to, literary people and architecture. Whenever I had an exhibition, he bragged about me to his friends but basically thought I was indulging a whim. "Why not go in for fashion or advertising," he would ask, "so you can clean up?"

Henry had been a top athlete at school and college, and when I wanted his attention, I'd discuss tennis. I played well enough, but his efforts to make me into a champion failed. I simply did not have what he thought of as his "killer instinct." We dipped into each other's lives now and then, occasionally seeing eye to eye, but except for one brouhaha involving money (after which he didn't speak to me for two years), we maintained a wary affection. Then came a development which made our little skirmishes seem inconsequential.

At Bang Bang in 1960

He loved his bonefishing camp, Bang Bang, his own creation and, for fifteen years, his escape from the social swirl of Nassau.

Henry
c. 1956

Sometime in 1958, his wife being absent, he asked me to accompany him to a conference with his cardiologist in New York at which I learned that he had a serious mitral valve disorder: a heart problem I was myself to cope with many years later.

With devotion and an appropriately light touch, his brother Stewart, and Stewart's wife took care of him in their house in Stamford. I was a frequent visitor, and despite his condition, we found more to laugh about and closer companionship than in all the years before. He cleared up many puzzles of my childhood, telling me, among other things, that when they had separated, Mother proposed putting me up for adoption by Grandma Bacon's sister, Jeanette Marks, or Grandfather Thorne's brother, Brinck. Having grown up with my mother holding me at arm's length, hearing the news which once might have undone me now came more as a confirmation than a surprise.

Worried about his affairs in the Bahamas, he trusted me to check into them and to reassure the staff of his beloved fishing camp that he was being well taken care of and would join them soon. But within a few months, he had lost ground. In the summer of 1959, he became a patient of Dr. Dwight Harken at Peter Bent Brigham Hospital in Boston.

Dr. Harken, an army man himself, had been a pioneer in open heart surgery in World War II. My father had retained his title of Colonel in the Air Materiel Command. The two men took to each other instantly. With this unexpected camaraderie, Henry's morale improved.

Odds for successful surgery were small, but there was apparently no promising alternative. Fully aware of his chances, he elected to have the operation. It seemed to have gone well, but three weeks later, talking to me from his bed, he had a violent seizure. I called for help; his nurse and members of the surgical team rushed in. An eternity later when two of the doctors came to the waiting room, one of them said quietly, "We have lost Colonel Thorne."

I had lost him, too. But in the ordeal of his dying we found the respect and love denied us for a lifetime. Every year for many years afterward, in mid-July, I would catch a cold, become accident prone or depressed. Henry had died at sixty-one. When I approached that age, the first inkling of my own heart's disquieting rhythm haunted me with the thought that I might not live beyond it.

As generous in death as he was closefisted in life, Henry had ironically enabled me to pursue the very work he had dismissed and perhaps scorned. No longer did I have to take any random opportunity. I could afford to resume work on a film about Dylan Thomas from stills, and I could go on taking pictures of poets without concern for assignments or commissions. Henry's patrimony at once made my life easier, my career a matter of free choices. I am forever grateful to the evanescent stranger of my childhood who, in my middle age, became a father and a friend.

The Bang Bang Club
1960

As an executor, I attended to some of the personal requests Henry had entrusted to me, then turned to his affairs in the Bahamas. His bonefishing club, Bang Bang, basic and bare-board simple, was essentially a man's domain with accommodations for a maximum of eight guests. Set far from civilization in the North Bight of Andros Island, it was reachable with difficulty by a shoal draft wreck of a schooner, the *Headwind,* or more precariously by obsolescent amphibians, a Widgeon or a Goose. The ocean that passed through the bight was clear—the waters, colors of a Winslow Homer, pale green to aqua in the shallows to dark blue in the depths.

When I inherited the club, the Bahamas was still a British colony. Like many others of his holdings there, the cay had been leased by my father from the Crown when the Duke of Windsor, formerly Edward VIII, was Governor. It was still Colonel Thorne's property to those who had worked for him, and I was under tough scrutiny when I took over. The manager seemed to like me, but when we discussed club affairs, I knew from his inattention and averted eyes that he wished I would go home. My father's major domo, a strapping, mustachioed black man from Turks Island, addressed me with thinly disguised antagonism.

Even if they had welcomed me, it made little sense for me to involve myself in something so remote and specialized. After all, I told myself, I was a photographer with a developing career and, as a child of innkeepers, knew all too well the hazards of that occupation. Still, there it was—yet another playground to explore, too seductive to resist.

I took advantage of the opportunity to photograph black people who worked for us, sunrises, guests, birds, sea creatures—anything that caught my eye. Taking pictures from outboard skiffs presented no particular problem, but the coral surface of the cays was so sharp it easily pierced my tennis shoes. The guides' feet were tough as truck tires, and when, in envy, I asked one of them to let me take a close-up, he probably thought I was crazy.

Much that I saw happened either too quickly or was impossible to photograph: two large squid that squirted ink under water then danced along the surface like flying fish, tarpon choreographed to leap in unison, a bottomless, clear hole on a cay, dark water roiling in an ominous whirlpool in the ocean at the other "end" of the hole.

When the manager left and his replacement turned out to be unsatisfactory, I knew that, alone, I couldn't run the club from New York. There were, I reminded myself, other fish to fry at home, so I was pleased when an oceanographer offered to buy all the leases. A deal was made with wearisome deliberation and a heavy heart. Bang Bang was my last tangible tie to my father.

Gin-clear water and white marl flats in the North Bight made a perfect habitat for bonefish. Henry had taught me to catch them with spinning gear, light tackle and land crabs for bait. Easily spooked, hard to hook and spunky fighters, they were ideal gamefish. Since they couldn't sound in shallow water, nature gave them speed—"silver bullets," some called them.

Bonefishing

# *Artists*

My pursuit of poets came about by accident and continues by choice. Why, a friend recently asked me, had I chosen to photograph so many of them. A good question, for which I have no fully convincing answer. Throughout my life I have been drawn to artists, whatever their medium. While I have known and photographed more than my share of gifted people who in one way or another have destroyed themselves, I cling to the belief that the creative drive is life affirming.

To have a viewer say "that's a wonderful picture of Dylan Thomas" means more to me than "that's a Rollie McKenna picture." Not pretending to hide my own light, I prefer that it shine upon my subject. My way of shooting sometimes produces portraits of insight and sometimes "snapshots," which really refers to a technique and not necessarily to the quality or value of an image. Some of my most successful portraits are taken on the wing, some are lucky accidents and others the result of deliberate attention.

In an illuminating *New Yorker* profile, Dan Hofstadter wrote that the great, fine-tuned French photographer Henri Cartier-Bresson has been criticized, on the one hand, for overshooting and on the other, for professing to have extrasensory powers, as implied in the title of his book *The Decisive Moment.* (It was first published in France as *Images à la Sauvette* meaning, literally, "images in a hurry or furtively.") Actually, he rarely made more than half a dozen shots of a single subject, although he did take a phenomenal number of photographs on any given day. No matter how neurally and optically alert a photographer may be, that moment has already passed when decisiveness reaches consciousness, the shutter is released and the image registered on film. Cartier-Bresson would be the first to say that he possesses no magic, but might admit to a highly developed reflex system and a keen eye for composition. Yet there are bloopers even on *his* contact sheets.

I have often been asked how many exposures I take of any particular subject. My answer is: "Pick a number from one to a hundred." Of course this is exaggeration. I would rather it be as few as necessary. But overshooting, however defined, has its uses. Sometimes it has the effect of warming up a wary subject. Often it is advisable to take at least two rolls and develop one at a time in case of darkroom mishap. After a long session with someone uncomfortable about being photographed, I save a few exposures to shoot unexpectedly just when we both agree to call it a day. And what about the shot I thought would be great and turned out to be a bummer? Then it's handy to have another choice. And it can work the other way. After observing a person over weeks, days or even a few minutes, I may see something I hope to reveal, but come away dispirited because I've not caught it. Nonetheless, when the contact prints are before me, *voilà!*

However many exposures I make, it's important to me to give my subject a loose rein and myself all the awareness, openness and concentration I can muster. It's the result, not the method that counts, for when the actual shooting is over and done, another "decisive moment" occurs—editing.

Occasionally I give photographs away, but sometimes rec-ompense comes anyway—in the most unexpected forms. In the spring of 1951 I stopped at the studio of Marino Marini in Milan with an introduction from the artist Hugo Weber. Almost a year later, a letter came from a friend of Marino to whom he had given a photograph I had taken:

*Pieve Ligura, 25–2–52*

*Dear Lady . . . I thank you very much for it . . . I hope to see you again, and also—for this occasion—to offer you a piatto di spa-ghetti—plus Chianti.*
      *Hiero Prampolini*

On shelves in Henry Moore's studio in Hertfordshire, I noticed some soft stones with holes through them. Associating them with many of his sculptures, I asked if they had come from the white cliffs of Dover. "Oh, yes," he said, "I spent happy days there as a boy."

Following that summer day in 1951, he wrote,

*There must have been something in the air that made me take to your photographing better than I usually do. Our bronze casting is now turning out, after a lot of vicissitudes, very successfully. The first try we were about to make when you were here was nearly perfect. Now I shall do my own small bronze casting so I shall be able to experiment more easily than if I had to have them cast by professional casters.*

In bold, black handwriting,

*4 May 1958*
*Dear Rollie*

    *Why don't you come this week . . . If things are very busy you may get shoved around a bit . . . I will put on a clean red shirt.*
                            *Love,*
                                 *Sandy*

We went to Roxbury, Connecticut, a friend and I, and neither of us was shoved around. Instead we were treated to a superb lunch prepared by Alexander Calder's wife, Louisa, in a house where the pots and pans had spiral Calder handles and even the toilet-paper holder was his wire creation.

As I was leaving, Sandy said they needed passport pictures in a great hurry, so I obliged and produced two masterpieces barely distinguishable from police mug shots.

Covering the Edinburgh International Festival in the summer of 1957, I was surprised and moved by an event not an official part of the festival at all, but a performance On the Fringe. (Its closest counterpart, Off Broadway in New York.) Derek Jacobi—the now distinguished British actor and direc-tor—was making up to go on stage as the protagonist in the Leyton High School production of *Hamlet.* His performance so dazzled me that it was only afterwards that I fully took in the fact that he was only sixteen years old.

Cast as Captain Ahab, seventy-seven-year-old Erick Hawkins choreographed and performed in his own production based on Melville's *Moby Dick*. The premiere was at the Poets' Theatre in Cambridge, Massachusetts, in the summer of 1986. Under the hat, grease paint and heavy costume was a ruggedly attractive face and the body of an athlete.

On an exceptionally hot London day in the summer of 1969, expecting to find him alone, I met the poet Stephen Spender for lunch in Soho.

The beautiful young blonde with him was his actress daughter, Lizzie, above.

I have long admired the work of the British photographer Bill Brandt. His hauntingly beautiful *Literary Britain* remains one of my favorite books.

In the fall of 1953, provided with an introduction by Mary Lou Aswell, I telephoned him in London and was asked to come to his flat on Belsize Avenue. A shy, tall man, he appeared uncomfortable with his rangy frame, continually shifting his position as we chatted in front of the fireplace. It was like solving a jig-saw puzzle to fit him into his background, hemmed in as he was by paintings, vases, a telephone, a large bell jar filled with dried flowers and assorted bric-a-brac.

He seemed to relax as I began to shoot. When he received the two pictures Mary Lou and I chose to send him he wrote:

*I like your pictures very much, especially the profile, which is, I think, the best anyone has ever taken of me. I'm always so difficult but you seem to have made me forget about the camera.*

I preferred this photo; it shows more of his face, and the background composition is less confusing.

One of the most charming men I met in Brazil in 1954
was Roberto Burle Marx, renowned landscape architect.

John Piper lived not far from London near Henley-on-Thames with his wife and young children. His place, Fawley Bottom Farm House, was a combined home and studio. Known especially for his opera and stage set designs, he was also an accomplished easel painter. Like Bill Brandt, he was thin and lanky, but his movements were more deliberate and he appeared calmer, allowing for more leisurely picture taking.

One day in 1953, while browsing at Durlacher Gallery in New York, I fell for an oil painting of a black boxer entitled *Resting in the Ring.* Kirk Askew, the gallery's owner, suggested I meet its Italian painter, Titina Maselli. Struck by her dark beauty, I photographed her for the pure pleasure of it, with the painting in the background.

British painter John Minton lived with another painter, Keith Vaughan, in London. They, too, were recommended to me by Durlacher's. I photographed them both, but there was something so poignant about Minton (he ultimately committed suicide) I concentrated more on him.

I went with a friend to photograph John Osborne, whose play *Look Back in Anger,* at the Royal Court Theatre, was already a raving success and, in 1957, a generational landmark. While my friend was talking to his actress wife, Mary Ure, Mr. Osborne and I chatted as we decided upon a place to photo-graph. Inevitably, the already famous term "angry young men" came up. Mr. Osborne was quick to disavow any association with it. Just as we were leaving, my friend pointed out the license plate of a sports car parked in their courtyard. It read AYM.

Tom Wolfe. We began at my pied-à-terre on Fifty-fourth Street, but nothing there seemed appropriate as a background, so we decided to go outside among the newer skyscrapers on Sixth Avenue. Mr. Wolfe was a natural—full of bounce and confidence. For me to suggest where he might pose, or how, would have been an insult.

Responding to a request for a release of my pictures of him, he answered: *Did I ever tell you how very much I liked the pictures?*

# Stonington
## 1960–1975

### *Avenues to the Public*

Danny Jones
c. 1966

**B**Y SELLING the Bang Bang Club, I was free to get on with a life less divided and more focused. The sixties, so tumultuous for many others, brought me entirely unexpected professional satisfactions and personal fulfillments. Among them were the making of a film from my collection of stills picturing Dylan Thomas in New York and in Wales, and the acquisition of an extended family. Both events involved my childhood friend Danny Jones.

Since 1926, when we met at The-Inn-By-The-Sea, Danny and I had stayed in touch. Like my father, Danny had gone to the Eastern prep school St. Mark's, where he had won attention and kudos in photography, a hobby which excited him more than any of his formal studies. I had probably absorbed some of this enthusiasm for taking pictures from an early age. But in our late teens and early twenties, it was his charm that enthralled me—his skill at mimicry, his flights of fantasy and, most of all, his way, when we were together, of making me feel I was the most important person in his life, if not in the world.

Before Pearl Harbor, when he was in the Navy and I was about to sign up, we grew closer in the intense yet detached way of wartime associations—each of us afraid to give fully, commit or think of the future. At sea on the Murmansk run, he wrote often from the cruiser *Wichita*—long, half-fanciful yarns I wanted to interpret as love messages.

I responded cautiously, not daring to admit how deeply he had put me under his spell. Instead, I gave him news of our friends, his family and mine. As time passed and we became immersed in work and other people, our letters dwindled and eventually stopped. Only the family grapevine kept us informed.

Patricia Duell Willson
1962

I was married and living in New York when he returned from wartime service. Suffering psychologically and spiritually from his experiences, he retired to his mother's house in Newport, Rhode Island. Slowly, he mended there in the company of Navy buddies, among them Henry Solomon, who later formed the group at NBC which would produce one of the greatest of documentaries, "Victory at Sea." Danny was the unit's photo researcher.

After my return to Millbrook and subsequent divorce, we began to see each other again. He helped me refine what I had been trying to teach myself: intricate swings and tilts of a view camera, how to choose filters for various effects with black-and-white films, the way to pre-flash cut film to reduce excessive contrast. Unlike me, he was an endlessly patient and meticulous technician, and I strove to learn new disciplines.

Our old intimacy was not resumed until the year before my father's death. We contemplated marriage but also found that we liked our separate lives and so tacitly continued as before—he living in his Sixty-sixth Street apartment, I at the Eighty-eighth Street house.

Several years of separate living arrangements allowed us a large degree of freedom without loss of easy companionship. We both liked the work we were doing but, true to form, I was again growing restless in New York. *Hexel*, the boat I kept in Stonington, Connecticut, for weekend retreats, was cramped and, in spring and fall, cold and damp. Laid up in winter, she was no longer a substitute for living ashore. As a stopgap, I found a small apartment, and in 1961 bought a house on the edge of the sea—the very same sea that had been bringing the world to Stonington since the late eighteenth century. As much a legend as a place, it resisted an attack by British warships in 1814 and a few years later boasted that one of its sons, Nathaniel Palmer, at the age of twenty-one, claimed the continent of Antarctica for his country. The village's cosmopolitan makeup was still evident when I contemplated moving my base of operations from New York, which I thought then would be sometime in the nebulous future. From time to time, I more or less squatted in my new-found place as it underwent the serious face-lift it needed before I could call it a home. My work went on as usual in the city.

We were at a party in New York when Danny, temperamentally given to hyperbole, insisted that I meet an "absolutely wonderful" woman of his acquaintance, Patricia Willson of Flint Hill, Virginia. This time he had not exaggerated. Aware of instant rapport, we discovered, among other commonalities, that our mothers had left us in the South to be raised by grandparents and, in our absorption with childhood experiences, even found ourselves competing as to whose mother and father had had the most marriages.

Pat, I learned, had four children and a husband in Flint Hill, where she hoped I'd stop should I ever find myself in the area. Several weeks later, driving to Florida, I telephoned her and was invited to stay overnight. Deep in Virginia farming country, with rain obscuring the signs to Flint Hill, I finally identified the mile-long dirt driveway she had described as "almost impassable, but if you get stuck, just walk to the house and we'll pull you out."

There I met her husband, Freer, a tall, thin man, patrician and charming. The three children at home were asleep, the fourth and eldest in boarding school. We stayed up talking, drinking wine and listening to music until Freer retired around midnight. I needed sleep for an early start, but Pat was still wide awake. Picking up where we had left off in New York, we delved again into our respective childhoods, finding more and more in common as the wine flowed. We might have gone on all night but, with a long trip ahead, I gave up before dawn.

When I awoke to a foggy morning, Freer had left for work, and Pat had not yet come downstairs. A burst of giggles led me to the kitchen. When I stuck my head in the door, blond young Freer, aged ten (a replica of his father), politely introduced himself. Vicki, just a few years younger, played hostess by giving me coffee and toast, as Pud, only four, stared at me shyly with hooded eyes so like her mother's.

After leaving, I heard nothing until several weeks later when I was hospitalized with phlebitis in New York. A bouquet arrived with a card: "From Freer and Patsy." Danny must have told them I was ill.

Again, weeks went by without news from Pat. I was stunned when she called. She had left her husband, taking with her the three younger children. They were staying with old friends in Dutchess County not far from Millbrook, looking for a place to rent close to good public schools. Pat's and my conversations had dealt only with our past lives. Never had she indicated she was unhappy in her marriage, a revelation that also took Danny totally by surprise.

After they settled in Sharon, Connecticut, I saw them often (frequently with Danny) either there, in New York or in Stonington. As the end of the school year approached, Pat realized that she and her children had formed few strong ties in Sharon and that Stonington, smaller yet more diversified, also offered more accessible schools.

When a suitable house next to mine came on the market, Pat bought it and, in 1962, moved in. Defying friends' advice, we ceremoniously tore down the fence between our properties to create a large lawn we would share. For me this symbolized the beginning of an existence curiously akin to my youthful years at The-Inn-By-The-Sea, but with roles reversed. I was now a parent, not a child, in an extended family.

Gini, Vicki, Pud and Freer Willson
Pat's children
1967

Stonington, Connecticut
1964

This view of Stonington shows my house and Pat's in the foreground at the end of the last street before the point. I shot it from a plane not much bigger than the Piper Cub I flew in 1940, but this time as a passenger.

With Pat and the children settled in next door, I went to Stonington from New York several days each week. Then, in 1965, I took the plunge and moved—business and all. It was a wrench to sell the Eighty-eighth Street house, but my heart was elsewhere. As for my career, I knew I was taking a gamble, fearing that, so far from New York, I'd be forgotten in the fickle world of photography. (As it turned out, I took more photographs and contributed to more exhibitions than in the previous decade. Most rewarding, I got on with filmmaking.)

To stay abreast of business and to see Danny, I kept a pied-à-terre overlooking the Museum of Modern Art's Sculpture Garden and, in Stonington, bought an antebellum brick building in the commercial center of the village, hard by the old railroad tracks from Boston that once led to Stonington's docks and steamboats to New York. Gutted and remodeled to include three offices, a store and a duplex apartment, it offered me a studio and a spacious darkroom. Studio photography had never been my metier; but this vast building housing my photo files, equipment and books soon paid for itself and was the scene of memorable parties as well.

Pat and her children were very demonstrative with one another. I had grown up with little overt parental affection and, childless, found the love of children a totally new experience. It came over me like a warm blanket, but still my role was not always easy to define; sometimes second mother when Pat was indisposed or when one of the children thought I might be a softer touch; sometimes substitute father when her son wanted to practice basketball or her youngest daughter to learn to ride a bicycle. A buffer for everyone, I acquired not only a loving family but still another name—"O.M."—Other Mother.

The children seemed to adjust well to the absence of their father, visiting him occasionally on the yacht he kept abroad. Pat or I would accompany them to wherever *Joy King II* was berthed—Piraeus, Dubrovnik, Ischia—and continue on our way, Pat to Sweden, Hamburg or Italy where she had relatives, I usually to the United Kingdom or Ireland to pursue more English-speaking poets.

Pat, who had never held a job other than as a censor during the war (she spoke German), did well in a Stonington real estate firm. Her melancholy subsided as she put her divorce further and further behind, made new friends and invited old ones to visit the adjoining properties of what we had named The Compound, walled from the street and neighbors, open to Little Narragansett Bay. The common lawn and beach overflowed with children and guests in the summer. In quieter times we inhaled the beauty around us, a mutable ocean, nesting gulls on nearby sandspits and heraldic cormorants on the pilings, spreading their wings to dry. Distant buildings in Watch Hill lighted up as if on fire when the setting sun shone on them. In thick weather, the foghorns wailed, and in deep cold, sea smoke feathered off the water as the morning sun struck.

Pat
1964

Hedli and Louis MacNeice
1954

Already abroad, I decided to treat myself to a brief junket to Cork for another film award where I would see Hedli Anderson, widow of the poet Louis MacNeice, both of whom I had photographed in New York. After an afternoon screening of tediously didactic films, we drove to Hedli's home in Kinsale, where I spent the first evening in the kitchen of her renowned French restaurant shucking oysters as a stand-in for the kitchen boy. I might as well have been an adolescent back on Dauphin Island.

For years I had wanted to do a film on Dylan—but how? There was no film footage available. One Sunday afternoon in the late fifties I came upon a clue. When I tuned in "Omnibus"—a television program sponsored by the Ford Foundation—a short film made entirely from stills, probably no more than three minutes long, set me thinking. Why couldn't the same treatment be applied to a film about Dylan Thomas?

Danny, researching old stills for NBC's television documentary "Meet Mr. Lincoln," at once saw the possibilities. With his help, I assembled a rough print which members of Henry Solomon's Special Projects screened and patiently analyzed. Only then did I see how inadequate it was—dull, too long and amateurish. Why had I failed to realize that Dylan's magical voice was essential to breathe life into its dreary frames? Technically speaking, only by being shot on an animation stand could its jerky movements be smoothed out. Danny remained encouraging, but I had neither heart nor money to pursue the project until after my father's death, when I could afford to start from scratch.

Titled after Bill Read's book published the previous year (with the major portion of photographs mine), *The Days of Dylan Thomas* was not finished until 1965. Its first public screening, under the auspices of the New York Film Council, encouraged me—with much apprehension—to show it to prospective distributors in the screening room of Rizzoli's Book Store on Fifth Avenue. All the big-wigs I could rally, plus a carefully picked handful of Danny's friends and mine, packed the little theater. The music started precisely on cue; the projection was perfectly focused. As Dylan's story unfolded, I could sense that the audience was attentive, and when titters and laughs came, I relaxed ever so slightly. But when the twenty-minute run was over and the last chord sounded, there was total silence. I felt a flash of nausea as all my body's heat rose to my face. Tears, which I was determined to hold back, pressed painfully against my eyeballs. Then, when the lights went up, I could see that the audience had given way to its own tears, and I let mine go.

I was elated when Judith Crist called *The Days of Dylan Thomas: documentary creativity at its best.* Geri Trotta included it in *Harper's Bazaar*'s column "Not to Be Missed." Archer Winsten of the *New York Post* said: *It is a curiously touching memorial, at once objective and supported upon a foundation of poetic emotion.*

What the *New York Times*' Bosley Crowther said I either threw away or lost. But a copy of my letter to him says enough:

*23 March 1966*
*Dear Mr. Crowther:*
*Damn! No matter how hard I try I cannot extract an advantageous quote out of yesterday's review of* The Days of Dylan Thomas!

The film won many prizes at festivals. The Gran Premio from Bergamo provided cash that allowed me to fly to Italy and meet up with my Florentine friend of USIS days, Franco Giusti, who drove me to Bergamo Alta, where I accepted my prize in the deconsecrated basilica of Sant'Agostino. None of my fantasies about the reception of the film equalled this one.

*The Days of Dylan Thomas* was distributed for fifteen years in 16mm to well over a thousand educational institutions and film clubs.

Alluring as cinematography was, I had no intention of abandoning still photography. Exhibitions, with all the vulnerability such exposure implied, were hard to resist. They were also opportunities for self-evaluation and avenues to the public—and the critics!

The one-woman show of which I was most proud, People and Places, was hung in 1961 at the cozy coffee-cum-art Limelight Gallery in Greenwich Village. In a somewhat different version, the exhibition had been well received in Europe a few years before. But in New York I had yet to exhibit anything other than portraits and architecture, and I was eager for response on home ground to the total range of my work. Jacob Deschin wrote in the *New York Times:*

*The value of an exhibit for a photographer lies in the opportunity it affords him to show his versatility. When Mrs. McKenna turns from the portrait to the world scene around her, which she depicts in considerable variety at the show, it is on the same intimately descriptive plane as her approach to people.*

This was a real shot in the arm—my first photo review from a major New York critic. Just as it was a tribute to my available work, it was an assessment of my worth. If he had criticized my technical ability, I could have improved it, but if he had attacked my way of seeing—a mirror of my being—I would have been desolated.

The Face of Poetry, an exhibition of portraits of poets, opened in 1962 at the Firestone Library at Princeton University and traveled to twenty other institutions. The timing coincided with the publication by McGraw-Hill in 1963 of *The Modern Poets, an American-British Anthology,* edited by John Malcolm Brinnin and Bill Read. John and Bill had done some fast talking to convince the publishers that portraits would not detract from poetry. Nothing quite like it had appeared before.

With Howard Moss, John Brinnin
and Bill Read
1961

Louise Bogan
c. 1953

Joseph Brodsky
1990

It was a big academic success, partly because, as Louise Bogan pointed out in her *New Yorker* review: *People have enjoyed looking at photographs of poets and writers ever since Louis Daguerre "perfected" photography.*

In 1983 the Russian poet and Nobel Prize–winner Joseph Brodsky wrote in *Vanity Fair* that when he was in Moscow in 1968 or 1969, a friend had handed him *The Modern Poets: a very handsome book, generously illustrated with large black and white photographs—done by, if I remember correctly, Rollie McKenna.* On another occasion, speaking of its content and of how much it had meant to him, Mr. Brodsky told an acquaintance of mine that the book had been a revelation. Not only could he learn what contemporary poets in America and England were up to, but he could see for himself what each of them looked like.

A second edition was published in 1970 with several new poets and many updated portraits. There have been imitations since but none, in my view, with the same astute editing, and not one in which the portraits are the work of a single photographer.

As the seventies rolled around, my original family constellation was beginning to fade. Grandma Bacon's death in 1966 on her ninetieth birthday marked the end of an era. In 1974 Roger Generelly, my adored stepfather, died in Greenville, Mississippi. For ten years I had leaned heavily on him, often to the exclusion of my mother, simply because he filled a place she had never entered. We talked in our own language about *life*—such things as the feelings of others and how I behaved towards them—not about sitting up straight and keeping my room tidy. I knew, subconsciously, that he wanted to keep me as his child. But I was sixteen when they were divorced and, wrenching as that experience had been, I was ready to go.

I missed living in New York. But my sense of loss was mainly a frisson of nostalgia, an old familiar pang I felt when its skyline loomed up through the smog. My village and my new family engaged me more. To get to know the tiny peninsula that held less than two thousand souls couldn't have been more of a delight. In our small-town yet sophisticated way, we called one another by our first names whether we were newspaper vendor, retired Navy captain, druggist, ex-editor of a fashion magazine, poet or tough kid on the block. A heterogeneous bunch, we lived and let live. If one of us was ill, word traveled only as fast as offers of comfort or care. We gossiped, of course, but that was no more than local entertainment.

Photographing there, I was ignored when I poked around, snapped away at whatever intrigued me or set up my tripod and view camera in the middle of a street to take eighteenth-century and Victorian houses or the Greek Revival bank. Among my favorite haunts were the fishing pier where the Portuguese fleet was berthed and the marina which took care of my boat.

Twenty years of lugging heavy photo equipment had weakened my back and put an end to my tennis playing. Continuing my lifelong love affair with boats and the sea, I turned to *Scampi*, a twenty-eight-foot raised-deck auxiliary sloop I had bought in 1954. Her deck was so high the self-designated old salts of the harbor dubbed her *Layercake*. That year I learned to handle my first seagoing vessel and to navigate beyond the sight of land—considerably more demanding than teaching students at Gulf Park to sail small catboats in knee-deep water.

Pat's infatuation with sailing, compounded by mine, encouraged me to buy *Sub Rosa,* a graceful little wooden sloop with a rounded stern and a clipper bow. Designed by naval architect Gilbert Dunham, the boat had a unique feature—a hollow keel which permitted full headroom and comfort for two without the addition of an ugly doghouse. She was perfectly balanced, but I made her even easier to single-hand by re-rigging the halyards and sheets to lead to the cockpit. Pat and I cruised for a week or so every summer, usually in company with other small boats, as far east as Martha's Vineyard, southeast to Block Island and southwestward to Long Island.

Another sailor in town was the writer Peter Burchard. When he asked me to collaborate with him on a book about tugboats, I jumped at the chance. Boats and photography—to have a legitimate reason to combine what I liked most in the world was irresistible. Covering the port of New York and beyond, we boarded Moran tugs and met their crews, a special breed of men, physically tough but gentle in spirit. Some of them were grandsons of "hoggers," men who drove mules along towpaths as they pulled barges through the Erie Canal. Others were sons of "stick-riding" captains, as the skippers of barges were known. Many were of Scandinavian descent. Proud of their calling, all of them seemed to accept my presence aboard and my interest in photographing them. A night expedition carried us out towards dumping grounds off Sandy Hook with a "honey barge" in tow. Mercifully, the towline was a thousand feet or so long and the wind dead ahead. Both my shooting and Peter's research went so well that we found ourselves extending our story beyond its original premises. Our only disappointment came when, with a few hundred copies of *Harbor Tug* in circulation, the rest were destroyed in a warehouse flood.

Throughout the sixties and seventies, I went frequently to Europe, sometimes with Pat or one or another of the children. These excursions were the first I'd taken since 1948 when I wasn't driven to photograph, either by deadlines or my own compulsiveness. I took equipment along, but used it only when I was required to or particularly seduced by something. My camera had become many things: an inanimate object by which to earn a living, a maker of memories, a revealer of reality or a shield from it. At times it was my spinner of dreams. But on certain trips I concluded that, as an interceptor, a camera could also be an obstacle to seeing (in the deeper sense of the word)—an observation that may have enhanced my perception and curiosity.

With Peter Burchard
1974

We wrapped up our book with one of the crew taking snapshots of us and, a bit choked up, said our dockside farewell.

The power and precision of a little tug, whether nosing the nine-hundred-foot *Michelangelo* into her Hudson River slip or escorting the *Floating Hospital* in the East River, was amazing.

Tugboat in New York 1974

# Stonington

Twenty-five years ago, these pilings, remnants of a pier destroyed in the great hurricane of 1938, defined my view towards Watch Hill, Rhode Island. Time, tide and storms have left only the stump of one, invisible at high water.

My house, unlike many in Stonington, did not exist a hundred and fifty years ago. If it had, the view from a ropewalk near its site would have shown coastal sailing vessels loading up with beef, lumber and miscellaneous provisions for delivery to other New England ports. The water is shoaling, and only smaller boats navigate here now.

The following pictures were taken in the sixties and seventies, during the first blush of my romance with this extraordinary little spit of land and its inhabitants.

Summertime never lasts long enough. A cocktail party overlooking the harbor on a warm evening is an all too rare and joyful occasion.

On the west side of Library Square, the handsome houses, left, built in the 1840s, stretch for two blocks along Water Street.

A sudden squall in the harbor and a December gale battering my windows are warnings of the awesome strength of the sea.

What keeps me so close to the water is not just the physical location of my house but opportunities to photograph from my windows.

If there were an official Stonington bird, it would be the herring gull.

# Home and Key West
# 1976–1990

## *Circle of Affection*

Rollie and Pat
1969

Pat
1980

FOR ALL our experiences in common, Pat and I were very different. More European than American, she had spent much of her early childhood in Hamburg and Florida with her German grandfather and a grandmother from Virginia. In her late teens she lived with her mother and stepfather, Prince Nicholas Odescalchi, in Hungary. From there, at the age of nineteen, she made her way back to the United States after the Germans had annexed Austria and Great Britain had declared war. Unlike me, she had lost many people dear to her.

Publicly Pat was outgoing. She loved nothing better than late nights with friends, smoking, drinking wine and holding long conversations about Hungary, family and the meaning of life. But, linked so strongly to the past, she sometimes succumbed to a *weltschmerz* that was heartbreaking. Although I, too, loved "life-manship" talks, I was a nonsmoker and a light drinker—a pragmatist who liked to plan for the future. I think I was attracted to the dreamer in Pat, she to the stability she felt in me. Whatever the amalgam, together we formed, over nearly twenty years, a partnership the core of which was mutual devotion and the welfare of "our" children.

There was a whole new set of "rules" in society and the going for us all was sometimes tough, but we brought her brood safely through the tumultuous sixties and seventies with the aid of friends of ours and a handful of relatives. With the children now on their own, we planned a trip abroad for the spring of 1980; no working for me, just a chance to renew old friendships, visit favorite museums and relax. Away from domestic and professional concerns, we had a memorable four weeks. Soon after we returned, in a quiet moment alone, she told me she had been having chest pains. A biopsy revealed an especially virulent form of cancer of the lung.

Ann Taylor at Loch Ness
1981

Ann's and my connection went back to her birth when I was chosen by Helen Taggart Taylor to be her godmother.

What followed was eight months of nightmare, relieved only by Pat's immeasurable courage and the support of friends. The children's lives were in turmoil. But as they helped in their mother's care, they grew closer to one another, to her and to me. Her wish to die in her own bedroom overlooking the sea was honored on a bright, cold February morning.

I knew it had to be, but months of mourning left me without purpose or direction. I longed not to wake up early with the weight of grief and disorientation that kept me from concentrating on any one thing for more than a few minutes. Remembering the mishaps I had suffered after my father's death, I tried hard to keep myself in good physical shape—a task made more difficult by an unruly heart rhythm which was responding poorly to medication. Jutta, the long-haired dachshund Pat and I had bought in Germany, sensed something was wrong and never left my side.

Just when I was most depressed, two related events pulled me out of the doldrums: a trip to Wales with the artist Ann Taylor and the writing of *Portrait of Dylan: A Photographer's Memoir.* Visiting Wales not only spurred me to update photographs of Laugharne and Swansea for the book I had contracted to write, but boosted my sagging spirits. I returned home refreshed and eager to start.

Writing my recollections, with the aid of my endlessly resourceful assistant Judith Bachmann, forced me to concentrate as I had been unable to do for a year—even though a mild case of shingles threatened my "shooting" eye. As I wrote of the scant year I had known Dylan and the drama that all but obscured his death, I knew my tears were not for him alone.

An exorcism as well as a memoir, *Portrait,* published in 1982, was a *succès d'estime.* The writing of it alleviated my personal anguish and gave my photographs of Dylan a longer life than they would have in magazines and films.

The following year, Artists at Large, my first big retrospective exhibition of people, opened at Vassar. Curated by Mac Doty, Director of the Currier Gallery of Art in Manchester, New Hampshire, it circulated for two years.

Bolstered by favorable reaction to my work, the frequent presence of the children and the passage of time, I recovered somewhat from Pat's death. My health, however, was deteriorating, despite skilled medical attention, a less strenuous regime and winters in Key West. I felt better in the South, but my energy was low and, with exertion, breathing was difficult.

Equally disturbing, I found myself losing interest in photography as I had practiced it for thirty-five years. I wanted sympathetic professional guidance, not instruction, but where, from whom? Fearing photographic paralysis, my quest led me to the Maine Photographic Workshop and Lilo Raymond.

En route to Rockport, Maine, I spent the night with Danny Jones in Cambridge, where my car was broken into and everything portable stolen—tape deck, tapes, bicycle, clothes, tripod, portfolio, all cameras and lenses. It was as though I had been personally violated, but I pushed on anyway. Hearing my woeful tale, the workshop loaned me a Nikon body and any two lenses of my choice. Planning to do nature shots, I opted for a macro and a long lens.

We all met in the mornings and went our own ways each afternoon. As the class progressed I realized, as Lilo did, that I was more experienced as well as older than the other students. When the time came for an individual interview I knew I had come to the right person. She neither directed me nor minimized my concerns. A kindred spirit, a photographer near my own age, she had at one time been faced with similar decisions. Some of my pictures held up well in daily critiques, but as time went on it was the class members themselves and Lilo I was photographing. Without quite realizing it, I had gone full circle from close-up nature to landscape and back to people.

The black cloud began to dissipate. I returned to Stonington with new interest in my work and life in general. But my health was not good. My cardiologist at the New York Hospital decided to do another electrocardioversion—an electrical current to shock the heart back to normal rhythm. It had worked once before. This time, three shocks failed to defibrillate it. Still groggy from the last one, I awoke one night to walk across the aisle to the bathroom, as I had been doing for several days, not having been instructed otherwise. But this time the IV stand caught in the half-open door and went down, with me on top of it in a tangle of metal, bottles and tubes. When I regained consciousness, I was on an X-ray table. The femur had been broken. It took months to heal.

My prognosis, should I remain on medication alone, was very poor. I was in heart failure. With a diagnosis similar to my father's, I could have been frightened of open heart surgery, but wasn't. Although I was eight years older than he at his death, I had led a far healthier life. Techniques for alleviating my mitral valve problem had been perfected. There was only a 4 percent mortality rate. Also, I had been a patient with the New York Hospital's heart valve study since 1983. Just about everything there was to know about my physical state was on record.

My surgeon found one of the cords of the valve broken and others weakened. He repaired them with a prosthesis and took a stitch or two in another valve, the tricuspid, while a heart-lung machine circulated and filtered my blood. A miracle of modern medicine, it was the gift of all gifts—my life.

Lilo Raymond
August 1985

When I think of the photographer Lilo Raymond, I see varying shades of white: white wavy hair, smart, white casual clothes. I see, too, flirtatious blue eyes and a big, warm heart. And then I look at her beautifully composed high-key photographs of the simplest things and know why only she could have taken them.

Bel Bacon Pope
Rollie's mother
at seventy-five and eighty-five

Euphoric over my recovery and increasing energy, I wanted to dive immediately into the photographic autobiography I'd contracted to write. But my thought processes didn't knit as quickly as the rest of my body. Perhaps that was a blessing in disguise. Without a talent for leisure, I resolved to put it to good use. Digging back to recall events—my family and myself as a child—was something approaching self-analysis or self-hypnosis. Stratagems for recall would not work, only time by myself and quiet. Exhilarating insights unfolded in my waking and sleeping hours, but putting them into proper perspective was another matter. It took several months for the veils of my memory to lift and allow me to write.

I was halfway into the book when my mother died. Together for the ten years that she and Roger were married, we nonetheless were strangers for my entire life. I remember nothing about her before I was five or six except that she wasn't with me. Later, try as I might, I could never pierce the armor she seemed to wear in my presence. When we were together, I became faceless, devoid of personality. I told myself she loved me. But, except for an occasional signature in a letter, she never said as much.

Two weeks before her death, she told a mutual friend that she felt she had not been a good mother and looked forward to a long talk. I sat with her for the last time in the living room of her house in Lake Bluff, Illinois, nervous in anticipation of the moment I had craved since our days on Dauphin Island. Would this be it? She shut her eyes tight, tipped her head far back in a characteristic gesture, reached for the remote control of the television she could scarcely see or hear—and switched it on.

The day after Mother died, I read through some of Grandma Bacon's old letters and learned that my mother's childhood in a family of boys had not been easy. She had worshiped her mother, who responded then, as in the days I knew them together, with little affection. Was my mother repeating, entirely unconsciously, what *she* had experienced? I wept after her funeral for what we could have meant to each other.

*************************************************************************

Since 1984 I have returned to Key West every fall, not as a bird of passage, but as a sensible woman seeking to postpone her own demise. I knew people there and, never comfortable in cold weather, I needed to spend winters where the climate was warm. It was no accident that I chose the small tropical island that juts out belligerently between the Gulf of Mexico and the Atlantic.

Once a community of maritime wreckers, it is now a friendly city four times the size of Stonington, with the same charisma my village had in the mid-fifties—in Old Town, elegant architecture interspersed with houses large and small that have seen better days. Of greater diversity and wider contrast, Key West's main street has a brash tackiness that would make my Connecticut village blush.

From the privacy of a deck at the rear of my house I can, by craning my neck, see the sky all around; rimmed, to be sure, by houses, some of which went up only last year. Like most desirable places in this world, Key West is in the grip of progress, a euphemism for development, not all of which is positive. Less than a hundred feet from my house, a large, overgrown lot concealing a path nick-named "Dirtbag Alley" was bulldozed and cleaned up in a day, revealing its real name, DuPont Lane. It was a big improvement, but along with sanitizing goes loss of privacy, cover for birds and the small kingdoms of other creatures. Red-shouldered hawks no longer alight in my avocado tree, and the lizards that play dead when approached will not be tricking me for long.

When I go out of my minuscule compound, with its walled garden on the street and the "sea" (a very small, high-fenced swimming pool) to the rear, I see Key West in a capsule: across the street is handsome St. Peter's Episcopal Church, its congregation largely black; next door to me on one side lives a genial Englishman who owns the gay bar on the corner; on the other, a widower from New England who gave me a strip of land big enough to make my poolside us-able. Next to the bar is a *kiosko* so small it would go unnoticed if not for the aroma of Cuban coffee, strong and thick enough, I am told, to hold a spoon upright. A few steps away is a bakery owned and run by a French couple. I try, without success, to stay away from it. Also within view is a new restaurant with everything from *tubiko* (flying-fish eggs) to Japanese apple pie. A few doors away, a stylish store with imported European clothes matched only by Manhattan's Madison Avenue is crowded.

Last year a big parking area opposite the bar was awaiting development. At night it attracted vagrants and homeless men. In this town coke is not a soft drink or crack the sound of a whip, so Jutta and I didn't walk there. This year a top-flight sports store covers nearly the entire lot.

Marie-Claire Blais, the novelist
and playwright 1986

One arc of my circle of affection is filled with friends in Key West.

John Hersey, the writer, 1989

Shrimp Boat

A Kiss from Captiva
at Grassy Key, Marathon

The ocean and the Gulf are as clean, warm and colorful as they are in the Bahamas, but I resist keeping a boat. Instead, I go out to the nearby mangrove keys with Captain Vicki. Once a Navy brat in Key West, she knows the area intimately. A conservationist, she speaks passionately of every endangered variety of mangrove, every eaglet or baby osprey born within miles. In a piece of water where the dolphins know her, they come to cavort at the sound of her motor and strains of the Mozart quintet she plays for them.

After I'd been in Key West a year, I was given an exhibition of portraits of writers at the East Martello Museum, a remodeled fort. Attended by nearly all the subjects, who were also my friends, success was guaranteed.

Occasionally I use the interior of my small house to photograph new faces or redo those I have done before. Airy and white inside, it emanates a soft, clear light ideal for photographing people. For the past three years I have been occupied writing the book at hand, but my list of projects, if not its accomplishment, is long. Key West is rife with opportunity to photograph.

My senses come alive here, whether I'm protecting my hearing from the mating drums of ghetto blasters or drinking in the heady scent of stephanotis, jasmine, frangipani. My eyes never want for feasting.

There is vitality, along with an aura of *mañana* and a certain disposition toward lawlessness. I am hooked on the place—and, most importantly, on those in the circle of affection that embraces me and inspires me to continue to keep my lens cap off.

# *Continuum*

Photographing is my connection to the world. As I grow older, I identify more and more with the people I have photographed over the years. Although many are gone, we remain attached, and through my pictures, I share them with the world.

James Merrill the poet in 1953, 1969 and 1990

W. H. Auden didn't like being photographed—he suffered it. The early picture was taken on the fire escape of his
Seventh Avenue loft in Manhattan in 1951; the other in the
gloom of his apartment on St. Marks Place in 1969. The in-
tervening years had mapped his face.

I have always had a soft spot for the writer Elizabeth Hardwick. We had met in Italy about ten years before I took this picture of her in her New York apartment in 1962. Seven years later, on a picnic in Castine, Maine, we renewed our acquaintance.

W. S. Merwin regarded the camera as a friend. He made me feel that he enjoyed our times together both in 1960 and 1969. The pictures were taken in Manhattan.

Anne Sexton and I corresponded from time to time, but not about personal matters. Her poetry is frequently dark, but nothing she said or that I saw in her foreshadowed her tragic death by suicide. I met her first in 1961 at her house in Weston, Massachusetts, where she posed at her desk in the corner of the dining room, and again in the sunroom of Bill Read's house in Duxbury in 1968.

In early spring of 1951, I took snapshots of Robert Lowell and his wife of two years, Elizabeth Hardwick. We met over coffee in the Piazza della Signoria in Florence. For a more intimate portrait of him, we found a tiny alley near the embankment of the Arno where Cal—as he was called by friends—was shy and serious, but not impatient.

A photo session eighteen years later with mutual friends in Castine yielded the last pictures I took of him.

Richard Wilbur in South Lincoln, Massachusetts, in 1951. He was thirty years old. In 1986 he was the same warm, charming Dick who never objected to my photographing him.

Two years later he became the second poet laureate of the United States. He and his wife, Charlee, live in Key West and spend summers in Cummington, Massachusetts.

Barbara Howes and I became acquainted when I photographed her ex-husband, William Jay Smith, in North Pownal, Vermont. A poet, too, she posed for me in Millbrook in 1953 and again in Stonington sixteen years later.

Leonard Bernstein was finishing *West Side Story* in 1957 at the Osborne, one of Manhattan's most luxe turn-of-the-century apartment houses, when I photographed him for *America.*

Meeting again in Key West in January 1989, I found him considerably aged, mellowed but almost maniacally energetic. Because he was a warm man, we fell easily into a first-name relationship.

The next winter, also in Key West, he worked for weeks at composing, but drew little joy from it. As he gave me a good-bye bear hug, I remarked that he looked sad. "I was on the crest when I returned from London," he replied, "but since then I've just gone down and down. I'm going back feeling as if I'd accomplished nothing, well, very little." His mood was echoed shortly after in a *New York Times* review: *In the Sibelius, Mr. Bernstein pointed up the qualities that exert the strongest pull on him—tension, angst and nostalgia . . .*

Below the mother-of-pearl beads is an ancient Israeli shekel and the medallion Dimitri Mitropoulos wore when he collapsed while conducting at La Scala in Milan.

Lenny died at home in New York on October 4, 1990.

Thom Gunn, the poet, had changed his locale from London in 1957 to San Francisco's Haight-Ashbury in 1969.

The photo I took in 1961 of Alison Lurie was for the
jacket of her first novel, *Love and Friendship*. In 1986 we met
again in Key West, where she spends her winters.

John Berryman was hard to distinguish from his students at Princeton in 1951. In 1969, hoping for a new picture for the second edition of *The Modern Poets*, I found him in a Minneapolis hospital.

One morning three years afterwards, he jumped from the Washington Avenue Bridge to his death on the hard embankment of the Mississippi River.

The first time I asked Robert Graves to sit for me was in 1961 in the green room of the Poetry Center. But in 1969 he was sick in bed at his home in Deya, Majorca. Ruthven Todd, the Blake scholar, had arranged for me to see him, warning me first to take a present—nothing mundane or machine-made. When I handed Mr. Graves an artifact I had found in Taxco, I knew immediately it was the right choice.

© Cheung Ching Ming

P HOTOGRAPHY is the magnet that holds me together. I came upon it
through the back door when I was most in need of identity and purpose.

As I learned of the feast out there in the world, I reached beyond the scope
of my ordinary comprehension to photograph anywhere, anything, anytime.
Consumed and consuming, I became an addict.

It gives me a sense of power, not to use as a weapon, but to interpret the
force and frailty of life as I see it. I love to take pictures; an act both esthetic and
kinesthetic. There is satisfaction in coordinating muscle and sensibility—as with
sailing or executing a well-placed tennis stroke.

Even now, I await the results of a photo session with anticipation and a touch
of anxiety. The emergence of an image on a blank piece of white paper still
amazes me. There may be more throwaways than treasures, but the attempt is
all, and the incentive to try again compelling.

The photographic process binds me to my subjects, animate and inanimate.
In my files today, the hundreds of people—famous or unknown—are not tro-
phies of the hunt, but the reward of a quest to understand, to communicate, if
only for a moment. They are guests in my mind and heart.

# Acknowledgments

The many people who have helped me in my career have my heartfelt thanks. Too numerous to mention, they will know who they are.

I am especially grateful to Harry Ford, who gave me the opportunity to write and publish this book. He nurtured it gently and patiently along its sometimes tortuous way. Much appreciation to my publishers, and to Victoria Wilson for acute editorial advice, and to my keen copy editor, Denise Quirk.

John Malcolm Brinnin has guided me meticulously from the beginning. He saved me from many personal and literary pratfalls. Whatever gaffes and errors that may exist are entirely of my own making.

Ann Taylor, who designed the book and who labored long and tirelessly on this ecphrastic endeavor, has my everlasting gratitude. In great good humor, she encouraged and sustained me throughout two years of soul-searching and hard work. The book is hers as much as mine.

Elizabeth Eidlitz returned invaluable letters I had written on my first European trips as a photographer. She also introduced me to the Macintosh and, with my blessings, ruthlessly honed my English when I began this venture.

Ruth Adams Paepcke, once my photo-editor, outlined the structure for combining words and photographs. Her skill set me on the right track.

For their individual contributions to this book, I am indebted to Lisa Alther, Marie-Claire Blais, Victor T. Boatwright, Ted Danforth, Inger Elliott, Helen Generelly, Priscilla Howe, Amy Jackson, Art Kara, Mary Meigs, J. D. McClatchy, Dickson McKenna, Maria McVitty, Elsa Mottar, Eleanor Perenyi, Liz Shaw, John W. Shirley, John Streeter, Frank Taylor and Mary Thacher. Pamela Askew, James Merrill, Jane O'Reilly, Pamela Preston, Philip Stapp, Joseph W. Taylor and Charlee Wilbur have read part or all of the manuscript and applied their knowledge, judgment and affectionate goodwill to its betterment.

For her forbearing labors to keep me from mundane business concerns, I thank my resourceful assistant and friend, Judith Bachmann. Krista Torres, who lovingly guards my house and animals, has been of great help.

My family tells me they are happy that my distracted behavior is over, but wonder what will come next.

Rollie McKenna
*Stonington* 1990

# *Technical Notes*

As a gadget-happy photographer, I've lost track of all the kinds of cameras I've owned. But I do remember my first. It was an aluminum Pontiac Lynx II, bought in Paris in 1948. Made in France, it came with a Berthiot Flor f2.8/50mm lens and took 127 film, 16 exposures, 3 × 4 cm. Following it was a series of 35mm, interchangeable lens, rangefinder cameras: a Leica III F with assorted Nikon lenses adapted, then a Leica M 2, which was heavy but had the quietest shutter I have come across. I tried a Contax with an aluminum shutter for a while, but it wasn't reliable for a seaside dweller. A Pentax body with a Kilfitt Kilar reproscope attached to a 150mm lens was my favorite telephoto arrangement for years.

These cameras required the use of a separate light meter; at first a Weston Master V and now a Luna Pro. The early Leicas had a viewfinder which attached to the camera.

When the SLRs (single lens reflexes) appeared, I was quick to change over to Nikons, with an interval (when weight was a real consideration) of owning Olympus cameras and lenses. Today I use the Nikon F3 and the Nikon 2020, which purports to do everything but speak. When I am unsure about focusing, I depend on its automatic feature, but mostly switch it over to manual focus and take my chances. For less critical work I like the Nikon 500, sometimes spoken of as an "idiot's camera." Actually, it is a well-engineered instrument used more and more by professionals.

The old soldier Rolleiflex twin lens reflex is a camera I'll never part with, though I have given up a Hasselblad, which doesn't lend itself to hand-holding.

Most of my architectural work was done with a Linhof Teknika 4 × 5 view camera which folded into a compact package easy to transport and not too heavy. Of course, it required a tripod. Film packs with twelve sheets were more practical but I also used cut film.

Film has changed a lot since I began. My favorite Kodak Super XX roll film, hasn't been made for years. It had a speed of ASA 100 and little grain. Today I use Plux X at 125 or Tri X at 400. I rarely push it beyond 1000 ISO. The latest Kodak films, Tmax at 100 or 400 (TMY), are comparable but not identical—when I can't get one, I use the other. Currently I am experimenting with Kodak's Tmax 3200 (TMZ) which is invaluable for shooting in extremely low light.

Papers, too, have changed since my introduction to photography. Probably the most drastic innovation has been RC (resin coated) papers which dry quickly and have a glossy sheen. But I still prefer fibre-based papers and often wish for an old-timer such as Dupont Defender Velour Black.

# Chronology

## Solo Exhibitions

1951 YM-YWHA Poetry Center, New York
1952 DeCordova and Dana Museum, Lincoln, Massachusetts
  Three Renaissance Architects: Brunelleschi, Alberti and Palladio, J. B. Speed
   Art Museum, Louisville, Kentucky, and subsequent tour to twenty-one
   universities, colleges and, under the auspices of the American Federation of
   Art, other institutions
1953 Smith College, Northampton, Massachusetts
  Three Arts Gallery, Poughkeepsie, New York
1960 Fotografi di Rollie McKenna, Milan, Italy, and subsequent tour
1961 People and Places, Limelight Gallery, New York
1962 The Face of Poetry, Firestone Library, Princeton University, and subsequent
   tour to twenty universities, colleges and museums
1974 Image Gallery, New York
1975 Gallery f22, Santa Fe, New Mexico
1976 Tod Gallery, Stonington, Connecticut
1978 Trumbull College, Yale University, New Haven, Connecticut
1982 Books and Co., New York
  Artists at Large, Vassar College Art Gallery, Poughkeepsie, New York; Lyman
   Allyn Museum, New London, Connecticut; Currier Gallery of Art,
   Manchester, New Hampshire; Danforth Museum, Framingham,
   Massachusetts; University Art Gallery, State University of New York at
   Albany; Kresge Art Gallery, Michigan State University
1984 Killian Gallery of Sharon Arts Center, Sharon, New Hampshire
  La Grange College, La Grange, Georgia
1986 Rollie McKenna—Photography, Mystic Art Association Gallery, Mystic,
   Connecticut
1987 Portraits: A Literary Photographic Exhibit, East Martello Museum, Key West,
   Florida; Miami-Dade Cultural Center, Miami, Florida; Broward County
   Library, Ft. Lauderdale, Florida

## Group Exhibitions

1956 Latin American Architecture since 1945, Museum of Modern Art, New York
1957 Fine Arts Gallery, East Tennessee State College, Johnson City, Tennessee
Louisiana Fine Arts Commission, Old State Capitol Art Gallery, New Orleans, Louisiana
Seventy Photographers Look at New York, Museum of Modern Art, New York
1960 Photography in the Fine Arts, Metropolitan Museum of Art, New York, and subsequent tour
Art Center of Northern New Jersey, Englewood, New Jersey
1961 American Society of Magazine Photographers, Alsilomar, California
The Magnificent Enterprise: Higher Education for Women, Vassar College Centennial Exhibition, IBM Gallery, New York
1962 VII Photographers Gallery, Provincetown, Massachusetts
1967 Man and His World, Expo 67, Montreal, Canada
1972 Images of Concern, Neikrug Gallery, New York
1973 Welsh Dylan, Welsh Arts Council, Cardiff, Wales
1975 Women Look at Women, Lyman Allyn Museum, New London, Connecticut
1989 Writing with Light, 92nd Street Y, New York

## Public Collections

Museum of Modern Art, New York
San Francisco Museum of Modern Art, San Francisco
Yale University Art Gallery, New Haven, Connecticut
Vassar Art Gallery, Poughkeepsie, New York
Monroe County Public Library, Key West, Florida
East Martello Museum, Key West, Florida
Harry Ransom Center, University of Texas at Austin

## Lectures

1961 Short Course in Photojournalism, Kent State University
1966 Rhode Island School of Design
1971 "The Concerned Photographer III," New York University, ICP
1975 "Photographic Master Classes," Educational Telephone Network Presentation, University of Wisconsin
1982 "Artists at Large," Currier Gallery of Art, Manchester, New Hampshire; State University of New York at Albany
1986 "British and American Poets," Westerly Public Library, Westerly, Rhode Island
1989 "Women in Photography: Making Connections," Bryn Mawr College, Bryn Mawr, Pennsylvania

## Articles by Rollie McKenna

"James Renwick Jr. and the Second Empire Style in the United States," *Magazine of
    Art*, March 1951
"Why Can't a Woman . . . ?," *Yachting*, August 1957
"Dylan Thomas," *ASMP Picture Annual*, 1957
"Helen Keller," *ASMP Picture Annual*, 1959
"Free Wheeling Portraiture," *Popular Photography*, November 1960

## Articles about Rollie McKenna

"Rollie McKenna," Fred Ringel, *Modern Photography*, June 1954
"Poets as People," Margaret Weiss, *Saturday Review of Literature*, May 15, 1971
"A Portrait of Dylan," Bethe Thomas, *The Day*, New London, Connecticut, May 30, 1982

## Photographs in Publications

*Vogue, Harper's Bazaar, Look, Seventeen, Mademoiselle, Esquire, New York Times Magazine*
    and *Book Review, MD, Newsweek, Time, People; Sunday Times* and *The Observer*,
    London, among others
*America Illustrated*, USIA Publication in Russian and Polish, 1955–61
*U.S. Camera Annual*, 1953, 1955, 1957, 1958, 1960
*Lorenzo Ghiberti*, Richard Krautheimer, Princeton University Press, Princeton, New
    Jersey, 1956
*Renaissance Architecture*, Bates Lowry, George Braziller, New York, 1962
*The Days of Dylan Thomas*, Bill Read, McGraw-Hill, New York, 1964
*Dylan Thomas: "No Man More Magical,"* Andrew Sinclair, Holt Rinehart & Winston,
    New York, 1975
*Stonington, Connecticut: An Engagement Calendar*, 1973, 1976
"A Village as Hero," Percy Knauth, *On the Sound*, November 1971

## Films

1965    *The Days of Dylan Thomas*, distributed by McGraw-Hill Book Company.
        Recognized by the following awards: The Chris Award, Columbus Film
        Festival, Ohio 1965; Diploma of Honor, Locarno, Switzerland, 1965;
        Exhibition Award, Edinburgh Film Festival, Scotland, 1965; Gran Premio,
        Bergamo, Italy, 1965; Special Screening Selection, Cork Film Festival,
        Ireland, 1965; Bronze Bucranium, Padua, Italy, 1966; Golden Eagle Ciné,
        1966; Special Jury Award, Chicago International Film Festival, 1966
1968    *Dylan Thomas—The World I Breathe*, produced by Perry Miller for NET. Based
        on film *The Days of Dylan Thomas*. Won National Academy of Television Arts
        and Sciences honors for outstanding achievement in cultural documentaries
1969    *A Nice Kid Like You*, produced by Eugene Lichtenstein, distributed by the
        Group for the Advancement of Psychiatry

# Credits and Permissions

Unless otherwise indicated, all photographs were taken by Rollie McKenna.

Daniel W. Jones, the author's lifelong friend, adviser and ongoing technical guru, expertly restored old snapshots and portraits that otherwise would not be reproducible. Americo Giannicchi, renowned retoucher, did miracles with a battered print of The-Inn-By-The-Sea.

Photographic prints were made by Rollie McKenna, Image Photographic Services, Chris Burnett and Daniel Jones. Sal Lopes printed those of Harriet van Schoonhoven Thorne.

Grace Mayer of the Museum of Modern Art kindly identified members of the staff as they appear on page 170. In researching, Rona Ruub of the Museum of Modern Art Library was particularly helpful. Other libraries and archives used were the New York Public Library, the Stonington Free Library, the Westerly Public Library (in Westerly, Rhode Island), Special Collections at the University of Delaware and the National Archives Trust.

## Photographs

Photographs on the following pages are protected by copyright:

3: Henry Sanford Thorne, c. 1917: The Phillips Studio, Philadelphia, Pennsylvania

4: William Dennis Marks at the University of Pennsylvania, Portrait by Thomas Eakins, 1886: Washington University, St. Louis, Missouri

5: Henry Douglas Bacon, c. 1910: Webber, Brunswick, Maine

26: Portrait by Hal Phyfe, 1938: Hal Phyfe, New York, New York

29, 31, 32, 34, 36, 38, 44 (Photographs by Harriet van Schoonhoven Thorne): © Rollie McKenna

42: Arthur Rochford Manby, c. 1904: from *To Possess the Land, a Biography of Arthur Rochford Manby,* Frank Waters, The Swallow Press, Inc., Chicago, Illinois, 1973

58: On the pistol range, 1943: National Archives Trust #80-G-42542

125: At Dylan Thomas's Boat House, 1953: Pamela Askew

169: Edmund Wilson, *Esquire* Magazine, 1968: *Esquire* Magazine

221: With Howard Moss, John Brinnin and Bill Read, 1961: Gene Baro

238: Bel Bacon Pope: Gene Sberna

240: A Kiss from Captiva: Rachel Billington

269: Rollie McKenna: © 1989 Cheung Ching Ming

Photographer unidentified:

3: Rollie with her mother, Bel Bacon Thorne, c. 1920

4: Mabel Marks Bacon, c. 1910

5: Rollie and her uncle Bill Bacon, c. 1926

6: Roger Generelly, 1923

7: The-Inn-By-The-Sea, 1928

8: Rollie, c. 1928

9: Bill, and Rollie on Bill's pony, Bella, c. 1930

22: Claude Schmit, 1932

24: Bel and Roger Generelly, 1933

25: With Helen Taggart, 1936

26: Jack Hulburd, c. 1938

27: Victor Corse Thorne, c. 1940

55: In the Vassar Lab, 1941

57: Daniel W. Jones, 1940

59: Henry Dickson McKenna and Rollie, 1945

85: With Danny Jones, 1949

194: At Bang Bang in 1960

223: With Peter Burchard, 1974

235: Rollie and Pat, 1969

## Text

Unless otherwise noted, text in italics comes from the journals of Rollie McKenna and from her letters to Elizabeth Eidlitz. Other written material quoted herein is credited to the following authors:

15: Eudora Welty, *One Time, One Place*, © 1971 by Eudora Welty

68: Diana Chang, excerpt from *A Woman of Thirty*, © 1959, reprinted with permission of the author

79: e. e. cummings, "Memorabilia," e. e. cummings, *Poems 1923–1954*, Harcourt Brace, New York, 1954

91: Helen Wright, *Sweeper in the Sky, the Life of Maria Mitchell*, the Macmillan Company, New York, 1949

99: Oscar Wilde, from an unpublished postcard from Elizabeth Bishop to the author, April 30, 1973

127, 128 and 136: Dylan Thomas, *The Collected Poems of Dylan Thomas*, James Laughlin, New Directions Books, New York, 1953

132: Dylan Thomas, "Three Letters" from Dylan Thomas to Mme. Caetani, *Botteghe Oscura*, Vol. 13, 1953 ("boomed and fiddled while home was burning")

141: Elizabeth Bishop, from an unpublished letter to the author, May 16, 1955, used with the permission of her estate, © 1990 by Alice Helen Methfessel

142: Marianne Moore, from unpublished letters to the author, August 21 and 31, 1951, used with the permission of Marianne Craig Moore, Literary Executor for the Estate of Marianne Moore

146: Edith Sitwell, from an unpublished letter to the author, January 16, 1954, © 1990 Francis Sitwell

150: John Malcolm Brinnin, from an unpublished letter to the author in 1951 with the permission of John Malcolm Brinnin

152: Glenway Wescott, *Images of Truth*, Harper & Row Publishers, New York and Evanston, 1962

160: Aline B. Saarinen, *The New York Times*, November 27, 1955

172: Katherine Anne Porter, from an unpublished letter to the author, November 29, 1956, reprinted by permission of Isabel Bayley, Literary Trustee for Estate of Katherine Anne Porter

176, 178 and 179: Helen Keller, quoted with the permission of the American Foundation for the Blind

179: Ruth Adams, from an unpublished letter to the author, July 1956, reprinted with the permission of Ruth Adams Paepcke

199: Dan Hofstadter, *The New Yorker*, October 23 and 30, 1989

201: Henry Moore, from an unpublished letter to the author, September 29, 1954, quotation used by kind permission of the Henry Moore Foundation

203: Alexander Calder, from an unpublished letter to the author, May 4, 1958, used with the permission of the Alexander Calder family

206: William Brandt, from an unpublished letter to the author, November 14, 1953, used with the permission of Noya Brandt

213: Tom Wolfe, from an unpublished letter to the author, June 18, 1971, © Tom Wolfe

220: Judith Crist, *The New York Herald Tribune*, March 22, 1966

220: Archer Winsten, *The New York Post*, March 22, 1966

221: Jacob Deschin, *The New York Times*, April 23, 1961

222: Louise Bogan, *The New Yorker*, April 25, 1964

222: Joseph Brodsky, *Vanity Fair*, October 1983

258: Leonard Bernstein, *The New York Times*, March 13, 1990

# Index

*Figures in italics indicate a photograph*

*A Note on the Type*

The text and display of this book are set in a typeface called EHRHARDT, named for Wolfgang Dietrich Ehrhardt. The original types on which this version is based were in the Ehrhardt type foundry in Leipzig in the early eighteenth century, but were cut in the second half of the seventeenth century, probably by Nicholas Kis, a Hungarian who soon returned to his native country to set up as typefounder and printer. This revival of the face was first issued by the Monotype Corporation in 1938.

*Composition by Graphic Composition, Inc., Athens, Georgia*

*Printed by Van Dyck Columbia Printing Company,*
*North Haven, Connecticut*

*Bound by Bookbinders, Inc., Tinton Falls, New Jersey*

*Designed by Ann Taylor*